· THE ·
Ma CUISINE
COOKING
SCHOOL
COOKBOOK

THE
Ma CUISINE
COOKING
SCHOOL
COOKBOOK

Linda Lloyd ▪ Toni Mindling Schulman ▪ Patrick Terrail
and
Helene Siegel

RANDOM HOUSE
NEW YORK

Grateful acknowledgment is made to Michael McCarty for permission to
use the following recipes from his forthcoming book,
Michael's Cookbook, by Michael McCarty: Red Pasta with Grilled Lobster,
Grilled Chicken and Goat Cheese Salad, Double Chocolate Brownies,
and Grilled Quail with Confit of Onion.

Grateful acknowledgment is made to the following for permission
to reprint previously published material:

Harper & Row, Publishers, Inc.: The following recipes from *Cucina Fresca* by
Viana La Place and Evan Kleiman: Panzanella and Strawberries in
Balsamic Vinegar, Marinated Veal Chops, Red Pepper Neapolitan Style,
and Spaghetti à la Cecca.
Copyright © 1985 by Evan Kleiman and Viana La Place.
William Morrow & Company, Inc.: Recipes from *City Cuisine* by Susan Feniger
and Mary Milliken. Copyright © 1986 by William Morrow & Company, Inc.

Library of Congress Cataloging-in-Publication Data

The Ma Cuisine Cooking School cookbook.

Includes index.
1. Cookery, American—California style.   2. Cookery—California.   3. Ma
Cuisine Cooking School.   I. Lloyd, Linda.   II. Ma Cuisine Cooking School.
TX715.M113   1988   641.59794   87-43221
ISBN 0-394-55298-X

Manufactured in the United States of America

Book-of-the-Month Records® offers a wide range of
opera, classical and jazz recordings. For information and
catalog write to BOMR, Dept. 901, Camp Hill, PA 17012.

Designed by Debbie Glasserman
Illustrations by Laurie Rosenwald

To ESH, GLH, and DVS for making me "just taste it"
To DL and OML, my "guys" who tasted their way through all of the recipes
And to Willie, my small companion in good food and bad over the years—L.B.L.

To RM for sharing her knowledge and love of good food
To JAS for his incredible enthusiasm and support all in the name of research—T.M.S.

For Ted and Joey—H.S.

To the restaurant patrons, chefs, and restaurateurs of Los Angeles who make it all possible—P.A.T.

ACKNOWLEDGMENTS

This is a book of many voices, of many creative people who deserve special thanks:

To some of the best chefs, teachers and restaurateurs in Los Angeles who put us on the map with their creativity and dedication, who are truly the inspiration for this book: to Michel Blanchet, Renée Carisio, Cecilia De Castro, Celestino Drago, Michael Feig, Susan Feniger, Patrick Jamon, Evan Kleiman, Michael Kojima, Ed La Dou, Jean-Pierre Lemanissier, Bruce Marder, Michael McCarty, Jean-François Meteigner, Mary Sue Milliken, Antonio Orlando, Michael Roberts, John Sedlar, Leonard Schwartz, Piero Selvaggio, and last but not least, Roy Yamaguchi.

To Renée Carisio for unrelenting dedication to collecting all the information that was needed and for testing and developing these recipes.

To Christine Hall, the voice of Ma Cuisine, for her smiles and ease in keeping the typewriter warm.

To Mel Berger and the William Morris Agency for believing in us.

To Sharon Boorstin for her early assistance.

To Jon Hubbard and the Irvine Ranch Farmers Market for their support.

To Charlotte Mayerson, our editor, for keeping us on the right track.

To all our friends who tasted recipes for months.

And finally to the people who make Ma Cuisine work—our students! Many warm, sincere thanks.

CONTENTS

INTRODUCTION

The Ma Cuisine Cooking School was conceived in the mid-1970s by Patrick Terrail and Wolfgang Puck at a time when the West Coast lagged far behind the East in culinary innovation. If any city in California thought it knew anything about food, it was San Francisco. Los Angeles had only a few good restaurants and you had to search hard for common things like basil, thyme and tarragon. What was needed, Patrick and Wolfgang thought, was a cooking school that would be like a "culinary clubhouse," where chefs and cooking enthusiasts could meet and share ideas.

At that time Patrick's restaurant, Ma Maison, was already established and daily contact with customers made it clear to him that there was a growing interest in the local cuisine. It seemed like a good idea to give people a chance to learn how to cook their favorite Ma Maison recipes as well as dishes from other Los Angeles chefs.

Informality was the key. A small space next door to Ma Maison was transformed into a warm cheery classroom. Judy Gethers, a food specialist, rolled up her sleeves and started it all going. Almost immediately the school seemed to tap into something very exciting. A wave of culinary creativity began to build in Los Angeles. The California food scene, with its own particular style and its own wonderful ingredients, was coming into its own. The Ma Cuisine Cooking School turned out to be the perfect crossroad for these merging creative forces and ideas. Now, of course, the Los Angeles restaurant scene has become one of the most renowned in the country and these days, new cooking techniques and innovations tend to migrate from the West Coast to the East.

From its inception, the school was everything its founders hoped it would be. Prominent chefs taught at the school, sharing their recipes and ideas with their colleagues and with Ma Cuisine students. The emphasis was always on doing. Students were encouraged to put away their pencils and put on their aprons. Even the most timid among them succumbed to the "get in there and work" spirit. Students could be found with their sleeves rolled up, covered with flour, tackling pounds of pasta dough, trimming the newest vegetable, or deboning a whole fish.

In 1983, Linda Lloyd and Toni Mindling Schulman joined the school. The curriculum expanded to include many different cuisines and a more eclectic staff of chefs. In 1985, another school was opened in Newport Beach. This book is an outgrowth of all this activity. Our aim is to share the knowledge talented professional chefs have imparted at the school and to do it with a vocabulary that's familiar and comfortable. Demystifying gourmet cooking, simplifying recipes that appear complicated, and taking the intimidation out of cooking is what we've tried to achieve. At Ma Cuisine we often assure our students that there *is* such a thing as a foolproof soufflé and *no* such thing as only one "right" way to prepare a dish. The recipes in this book should be taken as a blueprint or a guideline, not as ironclad instructions. We have always encouraged experimentation and know that six different cooks preparing the same recipe will produce six variations on a theme.

With this thought in mind, we have compiled a collection of tastes and techniques that reflect the experiences of some of the finest chefs in southern California and the best of what they taught at Ma Cuisine. We hope the following recipes will be not only a source of accomplishment to our readers, but also a source of fun.

Linda B. Lloyd
Toni Mindling Schulman
Patrick A. Terrail

ABOUT THE CHEFS

Michel Blanchet is the man responsible for maintaining the impeccable standards of L'Ermitage's founder, the late Jean Bertranou. It was in the L'Ermitage kitchen, under Bertranou's watchful eye, that many of California's most innovative young chefs received their classical French training. Michel was Bertranou's longtime assistant, recruited from New York's La Caravelle, where he had been a lunch chef. A native of the Loire Valley, Michel prepares classic haute cuisine without regard for culinary fashions.

As soon as Sicilian-born *Celestino Drago* started working in restaurants after school at the tender age of fourteen, he was hooked. By eighteen he was head chef at one of the best restaurants in Tuscany. Since moving to California in 1979, he has brought an authentic touch to several leading Italian restaurants, including the popular Chianti Cucina, whose menu he designed. As chef-owner at Celestino's in Beverly Hills, he continues to bring his imprint to the authentic regional dishes of Italy.

As lunch chef at Ma Maison for four years, *Michael Feig* was best known for his inventiveness with fish. Michael is a graduate of the Culinary Institute of America and a Massachusetts native. He left Ma Maison three years ago to begin his own herb farm, Country Fresh Herbs, and catering business.

Susan Feniger and *Mary Sue Milliken* have an extraordinary friendship. In Los Angeles, a town where credits are everything, they share equal billing as chef-owners of two highly successful restaurants, Border Grill and City Restaurant. The two midwesterners met while working at Chicago's famed Le Perroquet, and joined forces in 1981 at the City Café in Los Angeles. Now, at the small Border Grill, they concentrate on the home-style dishes of Mexico while at the larger City they serve an eclectic blend of recipes gathered from their travels to India, Thailand and France, where they both worked. Bold flavors, unusual ethnic ingredients, and authenticity are their trademarks.

Patrick Jamon's career is like a condensed history of French cooking. A native of Valence, a small town between Lyons and Provence, Patrick got his first job at fourteen at the illustrious restaurant Pic. There, without gas or electricity, using the original charcoal-burning stoves, Patrick learned sauces and discipline. From there he went to Paris, where he met the twentieth century head on at the nouvelle cuisine restaurant, Vivarois. Now, at his casual Les Anges in Malibu, he enjoys the freedom to experiment that derives from truly understanding the past.

Evan Kleiman, chef-owner of Angeli and coauthor of *Cucina Fresca,* is a native Californian who fell in love with all things Italian on her first visit to that country at age sixteen. She went on to study Italian literature and film in college, where she also began catering to earn extra money. She was executive chef at Verdi, a local northern Italian restaurant, before opening her own café/pizzeria in 1984. Angeli specializes in the simple home cooking of southern Italy. Evan's clear, fresh style relies on using a few simple ingredients wisely.

Executive chef of the Chinese restaurant chain Mon Kee, *Michael Kojima* was born in Tokyo. He received a degree in economics there and became a master of samurai sword fighting before turning to cooking. After working as a purchasing agent in Tokyo and New York, he was invited by the illustrious Chef Wong, of Tokyo's Imperial Hotel, to serve an apprenticeship. From Chef Wong he learned the intricacies of Chinese and French technique, the two most highly regarded cuisines in Japan. The large Shanghai-Szechuan-style menu that Michael has designed at Mon Kee displays his fondness for seafood and a wide variety of ingredients and techniques not usually associated with Chinese food.

Ed La Dou got his early training flipping hamburgers at Woolworth's. He then turned to throwing pizzas at restaurants in his native San Francisco. As much as anyone, he has defined the California-style pizza. Recruited by Wolfgang Puck to become pizza chef at Spago, Ed later designed the menu for the California Pizza Kitchen restaurant chain. Just about anything goes on Ed's pizzas—from barbecued chicken to broccoli—as long as it is fresh and the combination works. He opened his own restaurant in Laurel Canyon in 1987.

Jean-Pierre Lemunissier, who became executive chef at Ma Maison in 1981, worked alongside the legendary French Chef Paul Bocuse, as his saucier from 1976 to 1979. While traveling with Bocuse, Jean-Pierre, a native of the northern French seaport Dunkerque, visited Los Angeles for the first time and decided to stay. He worked first as a chef at L'Ermitage and then succeeded Wolfgang Puck at Ma Maison.

Bruce Marder is recognized as one of the originators of California cuisine. At his casual West Beach Café in Venice, he relies on fresh local ingredients to prepare a variety of cuisines. The native Angeleno received his training at Dumas Père Cooking School in Chicago and worked at the Beverly Hills Hotel and L'Ermitage before opening his own place in 1979. At his second restaurant, Rebecca's, he serves authentic Mexican food, lightened for contemporary tastes.

Michael McCarty, owner-chef of Michael's, was trained at Cordon Bleu in Paris, as well as hotel schools in Europe and America. His philosophy is to use the best, most luxurious ingredients in the most simple and correct way, according to French technique. He imports fish and produce from New Zealand. And to guarantee consistently high quality duck and quail for local restaurateurs, he started his own poultry farm with his mentor, Jean Bertranou. A native of Westchester, New York, he owns a second restaurant, The Rattlesnake Club in Denver, which specializes in regional American cuisine.

Jean-François Meteigner is the twenty-eight-year-old genius who presides over the kitchen at L'Orangerie, one of Los Angeles's most luxurious French restaurants. He received his training at some of the best restaurants in his native France, including Troisgros and L'Archestrate, where Virginie and Gerard Ferry recruited him for their stunning restaurant, the place for grand celebrations in Los Angeles. Although every detail of the cuisine is orchestrated to perfection, the food never seems overworked, thanks to Jean-François's elegant light touch.

Instead of serving an arduous apprenticeship in the starred restaurants of France, *Michael Roberts* started cooking as a way to relax while studying musical composition at New York University. He soon decided he preferred the spontaneity of cooking to any other art. He then attended the Jean Ferrandi Cooking School in France and cooked at restaurants there and in New York before moving to California and becoming executive chef and partner at Trumps.

Leonard Schwartz, chef at 72 Market Street, is equally at home with native American dishes and haute cuisine. Leonard, a New Yorker, was a graduate student in psychology at UCLA when he decided to make restaurants his career. Bruce Marder, of West Beach Café, gave him his first job and he later perfected his techniques at some of Los Angeles's finest restaurants, including L'Orangerie and La Serre. When he and his partners, Dudley Moore and Tony Bill, sat down to design the menu at 72 Market Street, they decided they wanted a casual place where their friends would feel comfortable eating two or three nights a week. So the popular menu features American favorites like meat loaf, chili, and cornbread done to perfection, as well as sautéed pheasant and warm scallop salad with apples and almonds.

John Sedlar, originator of Modern Southwest Cuisine, blends the earthy tastes of his native New Mexico—chiles, cornmeal, and beans—with the subtle techniques of formal French cooking that he learned under the tutelage of the late Jean Bertranou. John founded his restaurant, St. Estephe, with partner Steve Garcia in 1980 as a classic French restaurant. After two years in business he decided: Why cook like everyone else? His ability to combine painstaking technique with beautiful presentation and earthy ingredients has brought admirers from all over the world to this tiny Manhattan Beach restaurant.

Piero Selvaggio is California's dean of Italian food and wine. Since opening his first restaurant, Valentino, in 1972, he has sought to trim the excesses of Italian-American cuisine so that only the pure tastes remain. His second restaurant, Primi, further refines his concept of lighter Italian cooking by concentrating solely on first course dishes. Executive Chef Antonio Orlando, who created many of the recipes at those restaurants, is now chef-owner of the much-acclaimed Fresco. Valentino has one of the best wine cellars in the country, featuring the smaller vineyards of Italy and California. Piero is a native of Sicily and received a degree in journalism from UCLA before entering the restaurant business.

Roy Yamaguchi's culinary style is a sophisticated blend of his Asian heritage and Western training—something he calls "California-French with Asian overtones." Roy grew up in Japan, where he decided at age sixteen that he wanted to become a chef. He attended the Culinary Institute of America in New York State, held assorted jobs in New York City and Los Angeles until he landed one at L'Ermitage as Michel Blanchet's assistant. At his ultramodern restaurant, 385 North, he creates dishes that are uniquely his own.

APPETIZERS

Artichokes Barigoule

Patrick Jamon of Les Anges

How to Clean and Peel an Artichoke

To prepare this dish, use *baby* artichokes, not the larger ones. Working with a heavy chef's knife, remove the bottom stem and slice about an inch off the top. Pull off and discard the tough outer leaves, and then remove the remaining pointy tips with scissors. The hairy part, or choke, need not be removed in small artichokes; the entire artichoke may be eaten. In larger artichokes the interior part, or choke, must be removed. To remove the choke, insert a knife with a curved blade and cut away the pale green and purple leaves in the center. Then, with a teaspoon, scoop out and discard the hairy part beneath. Always add lemon juice to the water for cooking or reserving artichokes, so they keep their bright green color.

Though he's cooked at some of the most elegant restaurants in the world, including the Michelin-starred Pic and Vivarois, for Patrick, nothing beats this kind of basic home cooking from Provence. To do this recipe justice, use the freshest vegetables and serve while the broth is still warm and aromatic. This comforting dish is a good way to start a dinner of your favorite roasted meat or poultry.

2 pounds baby artichokes
juice of ½ lemon
2 tablespoons unsalted butter
2 small carrots, peeled and finely diced
2 celery stalks, finely diced
1 leek, white part only, finely diced
1 small onion, finely diced
2 cups dry white wine
1 cup water

1. Peel and clean the artichokes. Set them aside in a bowl of water combined with lemon juice, to prevent discoloring.

2. When all the ingredients are chopped, drain the artichokes and pat dry. Melt the butter in a 10-inch sauté pan over medium heat. Add the artichokes and the vegetables; sauté about 10 minutes.

3. Add the wine and water, scraping the bottom of the pan to release the brown bits. Cook over medium heat for 10 to 15 minutes, depending on the size of the artichokes.

4. Remove from heat and strain the mixture, reserving the broth. Divide the vegetables among four soup bowls and reserve.

BASIL MAYONNAISE

2 egg yolks
1 tablespoon Dijon mustard
juice of ½ lemon
⅓ cup virgin olive oil
⅓ cup peanut oil
10 fresh basil leaves, chopped
salt and freshly ground pepper to taste
reserved broth

1. Combine the egg yolks, mustard and lemon juice in a food processor or blender. With the machine running, gradually add the oils in a slow steady stream. Add basil and salt and pepper; process briefly to combine. (See page 227 for further instructions on making mayonnaise.)

2. Transfer the mayonnaise to a mixing bowl and whisk in the reserved broth. The mixture should be the consistency of thick soup. Pour over the vegetables and serve immediately.

Serves 4

Chicken Scallion Spring Rolls

Cecilia De Castro of Ma Cuisine

Water Chestnuts

Fresh water chestnuts bear little resemblance to canned. The fresh variety has a distinctive sweet taste and crunchy texture compared to the bland taste and waterlogged texture of canned ones. Fresh water chestnuts are the size of small tomatoes. Remove their dark brown covering by slicing off the top and bottom with a small paring knife and then peeling. Look for water chestnuts in the produce section of your supermarket or in Oriental markets. Fresh jicama is always a good substitute.

These wonderful tiny, crisp rolls stuffed with fresh vegetables and chicken are an everyday food in Cecilia's native Philippines. At home she sometimes substitutes a combination of ground pork and shrimp for the chicken and mixes dipping sauces of chopped garlic in wine vinegar, or soy sauce with ginger and scallions. A variety of prepared sauces are also good for dipping: ketchup, Chinese mustard, plum and hoisin sauce (available at Oriental markets).

1½ pounds ground raw chicken
½ onion, minced
8 fresh water chestnuts, or 4 ounces jicama, finely diced
2 carrots, peeled, cut in half and julienned
3 scallions, white and green parts, cut in 2-inch lengths and julienned
1 egg yolk
1 egg
1 tablespoon sesame oil (page 93)
½ teaspoon salt
¼ teaspoon freshly ground pepper
½ pound won ton wrappers (available at Oriental markets)
3 cups peanut or safflower oil

1. In a large mixing bowl, combine all ingredients except won ton wrappers and oil. Adjust seasonings according to taste and mix until well combined.

2. To fill the won ton wrappers, place 1 heaping teaspoon of the mixture in the center of each. Fold over two facing ends to form a rectangle and then roll along the unfolded side to form a small cylinder. Where the two ends meet, seal the package by brushing cold water along the inside edge and then pressing the opposite edge over it. Stuffed spring rolls can be kept on a tray in the refrigerator for several hours or frozen.

3. In a wok or deep saucepan, heat the oil over high heat until hot enough for deep frying. You can test the oil by dropping in a sliver of won ton wrapper. If it rises to the top, the oil is ready. Add about 10 stuffed spring rolls and deep fry for 2 to 3 minutes, until well browned. Remove with slotted spoon and set aside to drain on paper towels. Serve immediately with assorted dipping sauces.

Yields 50 pieces for hors d'oeuvres

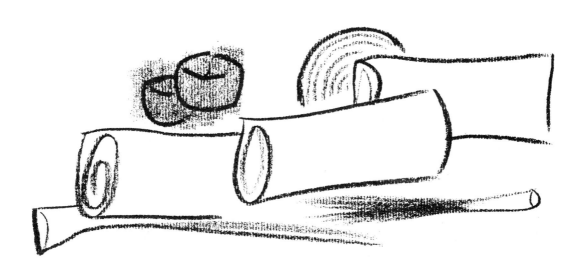

Green Chile Relleno with Mushroom Duxelles and Garlic Chèvre Sauce

John Sedlar of St. Estephe

When John Sedlar opened St. Estephe in 1980, after working for fifteen years in restaurant kitchens, he wanted his restaurant to be unique. He created Modern Southwest Cuisine, combining the classic French techniques he perfected under Jean Bertranou at L'Ermitage with ingredients he grew up with in New Mexico.

His cooking relies on the earthy tastes of chiles, beans and corn meal, but there is nothing heavy about it. His updated version of the familiar Mexican *chile relleno* is steamed instead of fried. The cheese filling has been replaced by a classic French stuffing of cooked, chopped mushrooms and the sauce, which ties the tastes together, is made of white wine, garlic and goat cheese.

The stuffed chiles can be made up to a day in advance. Place them on a buttered baking sheet, cover with a moist cloth and refrigerate. They can be steamed while the cream in the sauce is reducing.

4 tablespoons unsalted butter
2 pounds small white mushrooms, washed, dried and finely chopped
½ cup heavy cream
½ teaspoon salt
½ teaspoon pepper
2 (7-ounce) cans whole green chiles or 8 fresh green chiles, roasted, peeled and seeded
salt and freshly ground pepper to taste

1. To make the stuffing (*duxelles*): Melt the butter in a large skillet over medium-high heat. Add the mushrooms and cook until the liquid evaporates, about 25 to 30 minutes. Whisk in the cream and salt and pepper. Cook over medium-high heat until the cream is absorbed and the mixture is thick. Set aside to cool.

2. To stuff the chiles: Place each chile on a 12 × 12-inch sheet of plastic wrap. Slice the chiles open lengthwise and season with salt and pepper. Spread ¼ cup of the mushroom mixture inside each chile. Close the sides and seal with the plastic wrap by twisting the ends.

GARLIC CHÈVRE SAUCE

4 ounces dry white wine
5 large garlic cloves, finely minced
2 cups heavy cream
5 ounces soft goat cheese, crumbled
salt to taste

1. Combine the wine and garlic in a medium-sized skillet and cook over high heat until the wine is reduced by half. Add the cream, bring to a boil and cook until the liquid in the pan is reduced by half. Remove from heat; whisk in the cheese and salt. Reserve.

2. While the sauce is reducing, place the wrapped chiles in a steamer and cook over simmering water for 5 minutes.

3. To serve: Coat serving plates with the sauce. Remove the plastic wrap from the chiles and place the chiles on top of the sauce. Serve immediately.

Serves 8 as an appetizer
        4 as an entrée

Duxelles

Duxelles is a classic French method of cooking mushrooms. Finely chopped mushrooms, occasionally combined with shallots, are sautéed in butter and then cooked until all the moisture has evaporated and a very concentrated mushroom flavor remains. *Duxelles* can be used as a stuffing for poultry, fish or vegetable dishes, as a filling for appetizer tarts or *phyllo,* and can be added to sauces. For a stronger flavor, use mushrooms such as *shiitake* or chanterelles.

Corn Crepes with Shiitake Mushrooms and Asparagus

Antonio Orlando of Primi

When Piero Selvaggio, owner of Valentino, decided to open a second restaurant, Primi, specializing in first courses and desserts, he and Antonio spent three months experimenting with a wide range of *antipasti*, pasta and salads.

These corn crepes stuffed with a rich mixture of mushrooms and asparagus are a wonderful example of the style they chose. Instead of fresh *shiitake*, you can substitute 1 pound of white mushrooms plus 2 ounces of dry *shiitake* or *porcini* for extra flavor. You can prepare the stuffed crepes in advance and keep them in the refrigerator for up to four days. Just pour some cream in the bottom of the pan and reheat for 10 minutes in a 350°F oven.

CREPE BATTER

1¾ cups all-purpose flour
1½ cups cornmeal
½ teaspoon freshly ground nutmeg
½ teaspoon salt
3 cups milk
4 eggs
2 egg yolks
½ cup vegetable oil

1. Mix the flour, cornmeal, nutmeg and salt in a large bowl until blended.
2. Gradually whisk in the milk until smooth. Whisk in the eggs, egg yolks and oil until smooth; reserve. Unlike most crepe batters this one does not need to rest.

MUSHROOM AND ASPARAGUS FILLING

1 tablespoon unsalted butter
1 tablespoon olive oil
½ onion, finely chopped
1 pound asparagus, cooked and finely chopped
1 pound fresh shiitake mushrooms, stems removed and finely chopped
1 cup dry white wine
3 cups heavy cream
1 tablespoon fresh Italian parsley, finely chopped
½ teaspoon salt
¼ teaspoon pepper
2 egg yolks
1 cup Parmesan cheese, freshly grated
2 tablespoons unsalted butter for crepe making

1. Heat 1 tablespoon each of butter and oil in a large skillet over medium-high heat. Sauté the onions until golden, about 5 minutes. Add the asparagus and sauté for 3 minutes. Add the mushrooms and sauté an additional 3 minutes.

2. Pour in the wine; raise the heat to high and cook for 1 minute. Add the cream, parsley, salt and pepper; cook until the liquid in the pan is reduced by half, about 10 minutes.

3. Remove from heat. Stir in the egg yolks and Parmesan cheese; reserve.

4. To make the crepes: Melt 2 tablespoons butter over medium heat in a 9-inch crepe pan or skillet. When the pan is hot pour in ¼ cup of batter, tilting the pan to coat the bottom. When the top of the crepe looks dry, flip to cook the other side. Total cooking time for each crepe should be about 2 minutes. Stack the finished crepes between sheets of waxed paper.

5. Preheat oven to 350°F.

6. To fill the crepes: Spoon a heaping tablespoon of filling in the center of each and fold in half, and half again, so that the crepe looks like a quarter circle. Place the stuffed crepes in two 9 × 13-inch baking pans. Sprinkle with additional Parmesan cheese and bake for 3 minutes. Then place under broiler for 3 minutes or until lightly browned.

Makes 24 crepes

Eggplant Rolls Stuffed with Goat Cheese

Antonio Orlando of Valentino

Cooking Eggplant
Successfully

Eggplant contains a lot of moisture
and tends to be bitter. It also has a
tendency to soak up extraordinary
amounts of oil or butter when
sautéed. Salting and draining the
eggplant before cooking diminish
these problems.
Buy only firm, shiny eggplants,
free of wrinkles and blemishes.
Store them in a cool place for no
more than a day or two before
cooking.
When sautéing, use only
enough oil to coat the bottom of
the pan, and be sure the pan is
quite hot when adding the
eggplant. Turn the eggplant slices,
being sure to coat both sides
evenly with oil. After sautéing,
drain slices once more on paper
towels.

This sautéed and marinated eggplant recipe is typical of the kind of cooking Antonio grew up with in Sicily. It's full of flavor, from the hearty eggplant to the pungent goat cheese and garlicky vinaigrette. Antonio recommends making it in advance, a minimum of one day and up to four days. Remove from the refrigerator two hours before serving, to return to room temperature. Eggplant rolls would be lovely with Red Peppers Neapolitan Style (page 14), assorted cold cuts, olives and other marinated vegetables for an *antipasto* first course.

2 medium eggplants
1 teaspoon salt
1½ cups olive oil
8 ounces goat cheese, Caprini or Montrachet
⅓ cup red wine vinegar
2 garlic cloves, minced
⅓ cup Italian parsley, stems removed and chopped
⅓ cup fresh basil, stems removed and chopped
salt and freshly ground pepper to taste

1. Slice unpeeled eggplant lengthwise into ⅜-inch thick slices, sprinkle with salt, and drain on paper towels for at least 30 minutes. Pat slices dry.

2. Heat 2 tablespoons of the olive oil in a large sauté pan. Add ¼ of the eggplant slices and sauté until golden brown, 2 to 3 minutes per side. Remove and drain on paper towels. Sauté the remaining eggplant slices, adding 2 tablespoons of olive oil with each batch. Drain slices on paper towels.

3. Spread each slice of eggplant with 1 tablespoon of cheese and roll into a cylinder. Place rolls, seam side down, in a shallow glass or ceramic dish.

4. In a small bowl, whisk the remaining olive oil, vinegar, garlic, parsley and basil. Season with salt and pepper to taste and pour over the eggplant rolls to marinate.

5. Chill at least 24 hours and serve at room temperature.

Serves 6

Gorgonzola and Sweet Onions in Phyllo

Renée Carisio of Ma Cuisine

Caramelized red onions, creamy sweet Gorgonzola and toasted walnuts make a wonderful savory filling for delicate *phyllo* triangles. Once you stuff the triangles they can be stored in plastic bags and frozen indefinitely. Remove as many as you need from the freezer about 1 hour before baking. *Dolce latte* is an Italian blue cheese with a distinctive sweet, mild flavor. For more information on blue cheeses, see page 78.

1 cup (2 sticks) unsalted butter
3 red onions, thinly sliced
6 ounces gorgonzola dolce latte, *crumbled*
¾ cup walnuts, toasted (page 206) and chopped
8 sheets phyllo, *fresh or frozen*
¾ cup dry fine bread crumbs

1. Melt 3 tablespoons of the butter in a medium skillet over medium heat. Sauté the onions about ½ hour, until they turn brown. Remove from heat. Stir in the Gorgonzola and walnuts; reserve.

2. Preheat oven to 375°F. Have ready a buttered baking sheet. Wrap the *phyllo* in a damp towel and place close by. Melt the remaining butter and set aside.

3. To make the triangles: Place 1 sheet of *phyllo* directly on a counter. The reserved dough should remain wrapped. Cut the sheet into thirds lengthwise, with a sharp knife. Brush the strips lightly with butter and sprinkle each with ½ tablespoon of bread crumbs.

4. Fold each strip in half lengthwise and place 1 tablespoon of filling in the bottom right corner. As if you were folding a flag, fold the dough over about four times along the diagonal until about 1 inch remains at the top. Brush the flap with butter and press down to seal the resulting triangle. Place the stuffed triangles on the buttered baking sheet and prepare the remaining triangles.

5. Bake for 15 to 20 minutes, or until golden brown. Set aside to cool for 15 minutes before serving.

Yields 24 triangles

Fresh Versus Frozen Phyllo
We recommend using fresh *phyllo,* if at all possible, since it is easier to work with and tastes better. Look for it at Greek or Middle Eastern markets. It can be stored in the refrigerator for up to five days.

When shopping for frozen *phyllo* in your supermarket's pastry department, open the package and check the dough's edges. If they are torn or brittle, it indicates that the dough has already been thawed and refrozen on its way to market. Don't buy it; it will not handle well.

Steamed Mussels with Saffron and Tomato

Leonard Schwartz of 72 Market Street

The eclectic menu that Leonard developed for 72 Market Street is a reflection of his taste and that of the restaurant's owners, actors Tony Bill and Dudley Moore.

This cool appetizer of mussels steamed in wine and dressed in saffron mayonnaise is especially popular at the restaurant's oyster bar in the summertime. The directions for steaming the mussels can also be used for preparing plain steamed mussels or clams. If you plan to serve this dish as an appetizer, Leonard suggests following it with a simple chicken or pasta dish with the summery tastes of tomato and basil. It's important to use a light olive oil when making the mayonnaise since you want to avoid a strong, fruity taste. Please note also that because the mussels must soak before cooking and cool before serving, you should start this dish about 1½ hours before you need it.

1 tablespoon olive oil
30 mussels, cleaned and debearded
2 garlic cloves, minced
2 teaspoons shallots, minced
1½ cups dry white wine

1. To steam the mussels: Heat the olive oil in a large sauté pan over medium heat. Place the mussels in one layer in the pan and sprinkle with garlic and shallots. Pour in the wine; cover the pan and cook over medium-high heat until the shells open. This should take about 3 minutes.

2. Remove the mussels with a slotted spoon, discarding those that haven't opened. Set aside to cool. Strain the liquid in the pan and reserve for use in the sauce.

3. When they're cool enough to handle, remove the mussels from the shells, keeping half the shells for serving. Place the mussels in a glass or ceramic bowl, cover and refrigerate for a minimum of half an hour. The mussels can be refrigerated for as long as three days, if necessary.

4. Carefully wash the remaining shells in cold water. Pat dry and reserve.

TOMATO CONCASSÉ

1 tablespoon olive oil
1 tablespoon onion, minced
¼ teaspoon garlic, minced
1 sprig fresh thyme
½ bay leaf
3 tomatoes, peeled, seeded and diced (page 19)
salt and white pepper to taste

Heat the olive oil in a small saucepan over low heat. Add the onion, garlic, thyme and bay leaf. Cook until the onion starts to wilt, about 3 minutes. Add the tomatoes; turn the heat to medium and cook until the liquid from the tomatoes has evaporated, about 5 minutes. Season to taste with salt and pepper. Transfer to a bowl and chill.

SAFFRON MAYONNAISE SAUCE

reserved liquid from mussels
generous pinch of saffron threads
2 egg yolks
1 teaspoon Dijon mustard
juice of 1 large lemon
1½ cups pure, light olive oil
salt and cayenne pepper to taste

1. Place the reserved cooking liquid in a 10-inch sauté pan. Add saffron and cook over medium-high heat until the liquid is reduced by two thirds. Set aside to cool.

2. While the liquid is reducing, place the egg yolks, mustard and lemon juice in a food processor or blender. Process until combined. With the machine running, slowly drizzle in the oil until a mayonnaise is formed. See page 227 for additional information on mayonnaise.

3. Transfer the mayonnaise to a mixing bowl. Whisk in the reduced saffron mixture, salt and cayenne pepper to taste.

4. To serve: Arrange the reserved shells open side up on a platter. Dip each mussel in the saffron mayonnaise and place inside a shell. Top with ¼ teaspoon of the tomato *concassé* and serve.

Yields 30 pieces for hors d'oeuvres
6 appetizers

Tomato Concassé

By peeling, seeding and chopping tomatoes, you're making what chefs call a *concassé*, which can be used to flavor a multitude of dishes. It's a popular technique along the Mediterranean for flavoring soups, pizzas and sauces, and for adding a touch of color to grilled foods, shellfish and salads.

The technique for peeling and seeding tomatoes is the same as on page 19. Remove the skins to make the tomatoes more tender, and the seeds to eliminate excess water. Chop roughly and the *concassé* is done. Make tomato *concassé* in bulk and keep a supply in the refrigerator for flavoring summer meals.

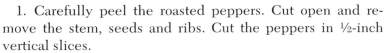

Red Peppers Neapolitan Style

Evan Kleiman of Angeli

Evan is often inspired by the housewives she meets on her frequent trips to Italy, who create a multitude of different dishes for their families with whatever ingredients are available locally.

This recipe, which she found while staying in Naples with Anna Folliero, the mother of Angeli's pizza chef, is a wonderful example of that ingenuity. The red peppers, abundant in Italy, are briefly cooked with olive oil, olives and capers to intensify their smoky, sweet taste.

This dish can keep in the refrigerator for about a week and improves over time. Serve either as an *antipasto* or vegetable side dish or take it along on your next picnic.

6 red bell peppers, roasted
½ cup olive oil
3 tablespoons capers
½ cup Kalamata or other good black olives, sliced off the pit
salt to taste

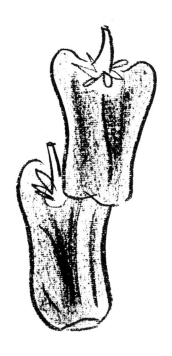

1. Carefully peel the roasted peppers. Cut open and remove the stem, seeds and ribs. Cut the peppers in ½-inch vertical slices.

2. Heat the oil in a medium-sized heavy skillet for 2 minutes. Add the peppers, capers, olives and salt. Cook over medium heat until the pepper juices begin to mix with the oil and the slices are tender, about 5 minutes. Serve at room temperature with toasted French or Italian bread.

Serves 4 to 6

Pork Picadillo Chile Rellenos

Bruce Marder of Rebecca's

To retain the pepper's crunchiness, this *chile relleno* is lightly sautéed, rather than deep-fried. Pork *picadillo* replaces the usual cheese. If the Mexican grating cheese called for in the recipe is not available at a Latin American market, substitute a light Parmesan or Monterey Jack. Bruce recommends a dry, fruity wine like Riesling or Gewürztraminer with Mexican food.

TOMATILLO SALSA

12 tomatillos, *husks removed and chopped*
5 serrano *chiles, stems removed and cut in half lengthwise*
2 garlic cloves, *crushed*
1 white onion, *chopped*
salt to taste

1. Combine all the ingredients except the salt in a medium saucepan. Cover with water. Bring the mixture to a boil, reduce to a simmer and cook, uncovered, until soft, about 1 hour.
2. Puree mixture in a food processor or blender. Season to taste with salt and reserve. *Salsa* may be made in advance, stored in the refrigerator and reheated before serving.

PORK PICADILLO

2 tablespoons lard or vegetable oil
1 white onion, diced
1 garlic clove, minced
1 pound ground pork
4 tomatoes, peeled, seeded and diced
1/2 cup currants
1 tablespoon red wine vinegar
1/8 teaspoon cumin
salt to taste

Melt the lard or heat the oil over medium heat in a large skillet. Sauté the onion and garlic until translucent. Add the

Peeling Peppers Without Baking Them

This is a good method for skinning a chile or bell pepper that will later be stuffed or baked. The peppers don't get as soft and smoky as those charred directly over a gas flame or under a broiler, as on page 14.

Place a saucepan with 1/2 inch of cooking oil over medium heat and heat the oil to deep fry temperature, 350°F. Drop the chiles in the oil, turning them so all surfaces are covered. Within seconds the skins will blister and whiten. Remove with a slotted spoon, rinse with cold water and remove the skins with a paring knife.

pork and cook until evenly browned, stirring occasionally. Add the tomatoes, currants, vinegar and cumin. Cook over medium heat, uncovered, until all the liquid in the pan is evaporated, about ½ hour. Salt to taste and reserve. The *picadillo* may be made in advance, stored in the refrigerator and reheated before serving.

CHILE RELLENOS

8 fresh green or Anaheim chiles or 2 (7-ounce) cans whole green
chiles
½ cup all-purpose flour
2 eggs, beaten
2 tablespoons lard or vegetable oil
4 ounces añejo *or* cotija *cheese, grated (see note above)*

1. If using fresh chiles, roast and peel them. Split them open with one vertical cut and carefully remove the seeds. Stuff the chiles by laying them on a counter, split side up. Divide the *picadillo* mixture and stuff each chile evenly.

2. Dip each chile first in the flour and then in the egg, to coat lightly.

3. Melt the lard or heat the oil over medium heat in a large skillet. Arrange the chiles in the pan, split side up, and sauté on three sides until lightly browned, about 2 minutes total.

4. To serve: Place two stuffed chiles on each plate. Divide the *salsa* and spoon it over the chiles. Sprinkle with grated cheese and serve immediately.

Serves 4

Potato Pancakes with Goat Cheese and Apples

Michael Roberts of Trumps

For Michael the kitchen has always been a place to relax, have fun and experiment with unusual combinations of taste and texture. These potato pancakes, which have been on the menu since Trumps opened, capture his whimsical style. The melted goat cheese and sautéed apples add a fresh new twist to a familiar favorite.

3 tablespoons clarified unsalted butter (page 167)
1 large Granny Smith apple, peeled, cored and thinly sliced
4 ounces soft, unripened goat cheese
2 eggs
¼ cup heavy cream
¼ cup all-purpose flour
2 tablespoons shallots, chopped
1 large baking potato
¼ teaspoon salt
⅛ teaspoon pepper

Cut Potatoes

Potatoes turn a dark gray color once they've been exposed to air. In any recipe that calls for shredded or sliced raw potatoes, it's important to work quickly once you've done the cutting. It takes ten minutes for them to discolor.

1. Preheat the broiler.

2. Melt 1 tablespoon of the butter in a small skillet over low heat. Sauté the apple slices until tender, about 5 minutes, and reserve.

3. Slice the goat cheese in ¼-inch thick slices and reserve.

4. Peel and finely shred the potato.

5. Whisk the eggs, cream, flour and shallots together in a small bowl. Add to the shredded potato and mix until combined. Stir in the salt and pepper.

6. Melt remaining butter in a medium-sized skillet over medium heat. Scoop quarter cups of potato batter into the pan and sauté about 3 minutes on each side, until golden.

7. Transfer the pancakes to a large ovenproof platter or gratin dish. Top each pancake with a slice of goat cheese and place under broiler for 3 to 4 minutes, until the cheese is melted. Top with the reserved apple slices and serve immediately.

Makes 8 small pancakes

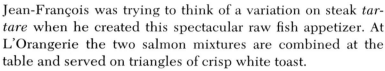

Salmon Tartare with Smoked Salmon Mousse

Jean-François Meteigner of L'Orangerie

Jean-François was trying to think of a variation on steak *tartare* when he created this spectacular raw fish appetizer. At L'Orangerie the two salmon mixtures are combined at the table and served on triangles of crisp white toast.

Serve with a dry, white wine at the start of an elegant dinner party. Make sure to use the best salmon available, to do his recipe justice.

1 pound fresh salmon fillets
2 shallots, finely chopped
1 tablespoon capers, drained and finely chopped
½ tablespoon onion, finely chopped
1 bunch fresh chives, finely chopped
juice of 1 lemon
½ cup heavy cream, cold
¼ pound smoked salmon, finely chopped
salt and freshly ground pepper to taste

1. Skin and trim the fresh salmon well, then dice finely.

2. In a mixing bowl combine fresh salmon, shallots, capers, onion and chives. Add the lemon juice; mix well and reserve.

3. Whip cream until soft peaks form. Fold in the smoked salmon. When well combined, fold in the fresh salmon mixture; add salt and pepper to taste and serve immediately with toast or crackers. The separate mixtures may be made in advance and refrigerated for up to five hours before you combine them and serve.

Serves 8

Seviche

Susan Feniger and Mary Sue Milliken of City Restaurant

Susan Feniger learned this marinated raw fish recipe on one of her trips to Mexico. It's authentic Mexican home-style cooking.

Always use a glass or ceramic bowl to marinate the fish—metal will impart a metallic taste. *Seviche* can be prepared a day in advance. Serve cold on lettuce leaves or tortilla chips. A great summer party food.

1½ pounds swordfish or red snapper fillets
¾ cup fresh lime juice
6 tomatoes, peeled, seeded and diced
1 large onion, diced
⅓ cup fresh oregano leaves, chopped, or 1 tablespoon dried
½ jalapeño pepper (fresh or jarred), diced
1 cup small green olives
⅓ cup olive oil
½ cup orange juice
1 cup tomato juice
1 bay leaf, crushed
salt and freshly ground pepper to taste

1. Dice the fish in ½-inch cubes. Mix with lime juice, cover and marinate in the refrigerator a minimum of an hour, or until the fish turns opaque. The fish must be entirely covered by the juice to "cook." Don't marinate any longer than necessary as the fish can overcook in the juice.

2. Drain the fish in a strainer, discarding the juice.

3. Place the fish and all the remaining ingredients in a ceramic or glass bowl; toss; adjust seasoning and serve. *Seviche* may be made in advance and stored, covered with plastic wrap, in the refrigerator for as long as 24 hours.

Serves 8 as an appetizer
    4 as an entrée

Peeling and Seeding Tomatoes

Bring a small pan of water to a boil. Remove the core at the top of the tomatoes and score the bottom with an X. Drop them into boiling water and cook for approximately 15 seconds. Remove with a slotted spoon and rinse the tomatoes in cold water to stop the cooking. With a small paring knife, remove the skins and cut the tomatoes in half. Squeeze the halves gently over a bowl to remove the seeds and juice.

Grilled Shrimp with Fresh Tomato and Garlic

Antonio Orlando of Valentino

This quick shrimp dish is an excellent choice for an elegant late night dinner. Serve it with a green salad, crusty bread and sparkling wine. The shrimp cooks very quickly—no more than 4 minutes on the grill or broiler—and the sauce is a simple combination of tomatoes, herbs and garlic cooked in wine. There are very few calories!

It's important to use the freshest ingredients and good quality olive oil. Antonio recommends Hawaiian Blue prawns or *langostinos* for the very best flavors.

8 jumbo shrimp, with shells
3 tablespoons virgin olive oil
salt and freshly ground pepper to taste
2 garlic cloves, chopped
1 tablespoon fresh basil, chopped
1 tablespoon fresh oregano, chopped
½ cup dry white wine
6 Italian plum tomatoes, peeled, seeded and diced
8 lettuce leaves, butter leaf or Boston, washed and dried
extra virgin olive oil for drizzling

1. Preheat the broiler or prepare grill.
2. Wash and dry the shrimp. Butterfly by slicing them open along the inside curve, leaving the shells on.
3. Brush shrimp lightly with oil; season with salt and pepper and place under broiler with split side up for 3 to 4 minutes. If grilling, place the shrimp split side *down* for 3 to 4 minutes.

4. While the shrimp are cooking, heat 2 tablespoons of oil in a medium-sized skillet over medium heat for about 2 minutes. Add the garlic and cook lightly. Add the basil, oregano and wine. Bring to a boil and cook for about 2 minutes. Stir in the tomatoes; cook an additional 3 minutes and adjust the seasonings. Remove from heat.

5. To serve: Arrange 2 lettuce leaves on each serving plate. Top each with 2 shrimp for appetizer, 4 for main course. Divide the sauce equally and spoon over the shrimp and lettuce. Drizzle with extra virgin olive oil and serve immediately.

Serves 4 as an appetizer
        2 as an entrée

SOUPS

Black Bean Soup with Salsa

Leonard Schwartz of 72 Market Street

Sweating the Mirepoix

The combination of finely diced carrots, celery and onion in quarter-inch dice is called *mirepoix*. It is traditionally used to flavor stocks, soups, sauces, and roasts. In black bean soup, the *mirepoix* is cooked over low heat, in a covered pan, until the vegetables are soft but retain their original color. This technique, called sweating, results in a delicately flavored mixture.

Leonard suggests making this soup the day before you serve it, since the taste and consistency improve with time. We think that black bean soup is a great choice for cooking on a winter weekend and serving throughout the week. It's satisfying enough to serve as a meal with some crusty bread and a salad. The tomato *salsa* is optional, but it adds a nice dash of color and coolness to the spicy soup.

1 pound thickly sliced or slab bacon, diced
2 cups carrot, finely diced
2 cups celery, finely diced
2 cups onion, finely diced
1 bunch fresh oregano, stems removed and chopped
2 tablespoons garlic, chopped
1 to 2 tablespoons cumin
2 teaspoons dried thyme
1 bay leaf
1 teaspoon freshly ground black pepper
1 gallon chicken or beef stock (page 224) or canned broth
2 tablespoons tomato paste
1 pound dried black beans, rinsed and drained
1 bunch fresh cilantro, or Chinese parsley, stems removed and
  chopped
1/4 cup fresh lime juice
salt and cayenne pepper to taste

1. Fry the bacon in a medium-sized skillet until crisp. Add the carrots, celery and onion. Cook, with the pan covered, over medium-low heat for 15 minutes or until the vegetables are soft.

2. Add the oregano, garlic, cumin, thyme, bay leaf and black pepper. Cook an additional 5 minutes.

3. Transfer to a large stockpot. Add the stock and bring to a boil.

4. Add the tomato paste and beans; reduce the heat to a simmer and cook for 2 to 2½ hours, uncovered. Check the pot occasionally and skim off the fat that rises to the top.

5. Stir in the *cilantro*, lime juice, and salt and pepper. Serve hot with sour cream and fresh tomato *salsa*.

Serves 12 to 16

FRESH TOMATO SALSA

5 tomatoes, finely chopped with skins and seeds
2 jalapeño *peppers, seeded and minced*
1 bunch fresh cilantro, *or Chinese parsley, stems removed and*
  chopped
1 bunch fresh oregano, stems removed and chopped (optional)
½ tablespoon garlic, minced
½ tablespoon freshly ground black pepper
¼ cup fresh lime juice
salt to taste

Combine all the ingredients in a bowl and serve as a garnish.

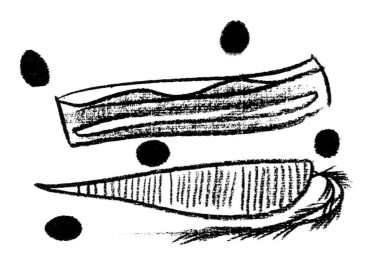

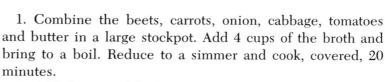

Borscht

Renée Carisio of Ma Cuisine

Seasoning Cold Foods
When cooking pâtés, ice creams
or cold soups—anything to be
served cold—always overseason,
because chilling diminishes
flavors.

This may sound like a contradiction, but Renée recommends this recipe for those who don't ordinarily like beets. Students are always amazed at how sweet and satisfying these vegetables can taste when fresh, rather than canned. Borscht is delicious all year round, hot or cold.

3 pounds beets, peeled and shredded
2 carrots, peeled and thinly sliced
1 large onion, thinly sliced
½ medium head of green cabbage, shredded
3 medium tomatoes, peeled, seeded and chopped (page 19)
1 tablespoon unsalted butter
7 cups beef broth
2 tablespoons white vinegar
1 tablespoon granulated sugar
1 bay leaf
1 teaspoon salt
½ teaspoon pepper
sour cream (garnish)

1. Combine the beets, carrots, onion, cabbage, tomatoes and butter in a large stockpot. Add 4 cups of the broth and bring to a boil. Reduce to a simmer and cook, covered, 20 minutes.

2. Add the rest of the broth and the remaining ingredients except the sour cream. Mix well, return to a simmer and cook, covered, an additional 20 minutes. Adjust seasonings and serve immediately or chill. Garnish with a dollop of sour cream.

Serves 6 to 8

Corn Soup with Red Pepper Puree

Michael Roberts of Trumps

The natural sweetness of corn and red pepper are elegantly combined in Michael Roberts's version of corn soup. At the restaurant the pepper puree is feathered in a delicate pattern that adds a lively splash of color to the pale soup. The chef also suggests passing around a dish of the red pepper puree for guests to spoon on at the table. This lovely summer soup can be served hot or cold.

2 red bell peppers, roasted, peeled and seeded (page 14)
8 tablespoons (1 stick) unsalted butter
2 small onions, chopped
6 ears of corn, kernels only, or 4 cups frozen
3 cups chicken stock
1 cup heavy cream
salt and freshly ground pepper to taste

1. Puree the peppers in a blender at medium speed until a thick liquid is formed. Reserve for garnish.

2. Melt the butter in a medium-sized Dutch oven or stockpot over medium heat. Add the onions and cook until translucent, about 5 minutes. Stir in the corn and sauté about 5 minutes. Add the stock, reduce heat to medium-low and cook, covered, about 15 minutes. Remove from heat.

3. Spoon the corn, with as little liquid as possible, into a food processor fitted with a metal blade. Puree until smooth. Pass the mixture through a medium strainer. Discard the skins and place the liquid and corn in the soup pot.

4. Warm over low heat; mix in the cream and season to taste with salt and pepper.

5. Ladle the soup into serving bowls. Garnish with the red pepper puree and serve immediately, or chill and add the garnish before serving.

Serves 4

Garnishing Tips

The key to creating a surface pattern with a garnish is getting the soup and the puree the same consistency. If the puree is heavier than the soup it will sink when you try to feather it. The soup will still taste fine. It just won't be as pretty.

To decorate in a feather pattern, spoon the puree in two lines on the soup's surface. With the back of a teaspoon or the tip of a paring knife, zigzag through the two lines. *Voilà!*

Sweet Lentil Soup

Michel Blanchet of L'Ermitage

Cooking with Beans
Before cooking with dried beans
it's important to wash them
carefully and pick through to
remove any pebbles or dirt. Once
clean, it is not necessary to soak
the beans since they cook until
tender in the simmering broth.
When soaking is necessary to
tenderize beans, we suggest
blanching them instead for 2
minutes. The results are the same.

Michel created this light lentil soup so that people could enjoy the classic progression of courses at L'Ermitage without getting uncomfortably full. It's the sweetest, most elegant lentil soup we've ever tasted. Michel suggests following his refined bean soup with a hearty meat or poultry dish like *coq au vin*.

7 tablespoons unsalted butter
1 large onion, chopped
1 large leek, white part only, cleaned and chopped (page 37)
2 tablespoons olive oil
3 large tomatoes, peeled, seeded and chopped (page 19)
1⅓ cup lentils, rinsed and drained
4 cups chicken stock (page 224) or canned chicken broth
2 garlic cloves, minced
½ cup heavy cream
1 bunch fresh basil, stems removed and chopped

1. Melt the butter in a large Dutch oven over medium-low heat. Add the onions and leeks. Cook until soft, about 10 minutes.

2. Heat the oil in a 10-inch sauté pan over medium heat. Add the tomatoes and sauté until most of the liquid evaporates, about 15 minutes.

3. Transfer the tomatoes to the Dutch oven and add lentils, chicken stock and garlic. Bring the mixture to a boil; reduce to a simmer and cook, covered, until the lentils are tender, about 45 minutes.

4. Puree the hot mixture in a food processor. Strain through a medium sieve and return the liquid to the pot. Stir in the cream and basil; warm over low heat for 5 minutes and serve immediately.

Serves 4

Minestrone

Renée Carisio of Ma Cuisine

This is a traditional recipe from Milan. Don't be concerned with the amount of stock. The pasta and potatoes absorb liquid as they cook. Serve this hearty soup before a traditional Italian meal of Osso Buco (page 129) or alone for a light winter lunch.

4 ounces salt pork, cold
2 garlic cloves, minced
2 tablespoons parsley, stems removed and chopped
12 cups chicken stock (page 224)
½ cup dry pinto beans, washed
½ cup dry navy beans, washed
4 tomatoes, peeled, seeded and chopped (page 19)
2 medium carrots, peeled and chopped
2 celery stalks, chopped
1 large onion, chopped
1 medium baking potato, peeled and diced
1 medium zucchini, chopped
½ cup elbow macaroni
¼ head green cabbage, coarsely sliced
salt and freshly ground pepper to taste

1. Chop the salt pork, garlic and parsley until a paste forms. Combine the paste, chicken stock and pinto beans in a large stockpot. Bring to a boil, reduce to a simmer and cook, covered, 1 hour. Do not stir.

2. Add the navy beans and tomatoes and continue to simmer, covered, 1 hour. Add the carrots, celery and onion; simmer an additional 20 minutes. Then add the potato for another 15 minutes, zucchini and macaroni 10 minutes and the cabbage 3 to 4 minutes, replacing the cover after each addition. Season with salt and pepper to taste and serve immediately.

Serves 8

Soup Vegetables

The key to making any vegetable soup is adding the vegetables in the proper order. Harder vegetables such as carrots should always be added first and softer vegetables like zucchini and cabbage last. Apply this rule to any soup or stew that calls for a combination of vegetables, to ensure that they all cook to the same degree of tenderness.

Oyster Stew

Bruce Marder of West Beach Café

This simple fish chowder cooks very quickly. There's no fish stock, and the cream and vegetable base can be made in advance and reheated. It's important to cook the oysters very briefly. More than one minute will make them tough. Bruce likes to serve this satisfying soup as an appetizer, followed by a simple grilled entrée.

4 ounces pancetta *or slab bacon, cut in ¼-inch dice*
½ onion, cut in ¼-inch dice
2 carrots, peeled and cut in ¼-inch dice
2 medium new potatoes, peeled and cut in ¼-inch dice
1 jalapeño *pepper, seeds removed and minced, or 1 teaspoon Tabasco*
1 quart heavy cream
2 tablespoons fresh thyme, stems removed, or 2 teaspoons dried
16 fresh raw oysters, shucked
salt and freshly ground pepper to taste

1. Sauté the *pancetta* or bacon and onion in a large saucepan or Dutch oven over medium heat about 5 minutes.

2. Add the carrots and potatoes. Sauté about 5 minutes. Add the *jalapeño* and cream. Cook over medium-high heat until the cream is reduced by one third, about 15 minutes.

3. Stir in the thyme and oysters. Cook long enough to just heat the oysters through, about 1 minute. Season with salt and pepper to taste and serve immediately.

Serves 4 to 6

How to Shuck Oysters

You need an oyster knife or a screwdriver to open the shell. With a kitchen towel in your hand to protect it, hold the washed shell, round side down, in the palm of your hand. Insert the knife or screwdriver in the narrow end, twisting it to open the shell slightly. Then slide the knife around until the top half can be lifted. Push the oysters out with your fingers.

Fresh, closed oysters or clams may be stored in their shells in the refrigerator for up to three days. They do need air, so store them in a bowl covered with a wet towel, in the coldest part of the refrigerator. Once the shells are opened, the oysters may be stored in their liquid, in a well-sealed container in the refrigerator, for the same amount of time.

Curried Squash Soup

Renée Carisio of Ma Cuisine

This pale orange soup is a delicate blend of sweet and spicy flavors. It's lovely to begin an autumn dinner of grilled fish or chicken or to serve at lunch with good, fresh bread like the currant-walnut *baguettes* on page 61. Acorn squash, carrots or fresh pumpkin may be substituted for butternut squash.

2 tablespoons unsalted butter
3 leeks, white part, cut in ¼-inch horizontal slices
1½ tablespoons curry powder
1 large butternut squash, peeled, seeded and sliced
4 cups fresh chicken stock (page 224)
¾ cup heavy cream or coconut milk
salt, pepper and freshly grated nutmeg to taste

1. Melt the butter in a medium stockpot or Dutch oven over medium heat. Add the leeks and cook until soft, about 5 minutes. Add the curry powder and cook an additional 2 minutes, stirring occasionally. Add the squash and stock. Bring to a boil, reduce to a simmer and cook, covered, until the squash is tender, about 35 minutes.

2. Puree in a blender or food processor until smooth. Return the mixture to the pot, pour in the cream or coconut milk and cook over medium-low heat about 5 minutes just to warm. Adjust seasonings with salt, pepper and nutmeg and serve immediately.

Serves 4 to 6

Homemade Curry Powder

The term curry powder does not exist in India, where each cook blends his own spices according to taste. We suggest you try our blend and use it as a starting point. You'll find the freshly ground spices add a rounder flavor to whatever you are cooking. All the ingredients can be ground together in a blender, coffee or spice grinder.

4 cloves
½ teaspoon cumin seeds
½ teaspoon white peppercorns
½ teaspoon mustard seeds
½ teaspoon powdered ginger
½ teaspoon fenugreek seeds
½ teaspoon cardamom seeds
1½ teaspoons ground turmeric
2 teaspoons coriander seeds
½ cinnamon stick
3 dried red Japanese chile peppers with seeds

PASTA & RICE

Spaghetti alla Checca

Evan Kleiman of Angeli

**General Dry Pasta Cooking
Instructions**

Bring an abundant amount of
salted water to a boil
(approximately 1 gallon of water
for 1 pound of pasta). Add the
pasta, stirring gently to prevent
sticking. Over moderately high
heat, bring the water back to a
boil and cook the pasta
approximately 8 minutes or until it
is cooked yet *al dente* or firm to
the bite. When the pasta is
cooked, immediately add a cup of
cold water to the pot and then
drain. *Do not rinse* unless you're
making a cold pasta salad or a
dish like lasagne. The bit of starch
that remains on the cooked pasta
after the water is drained helps the
sauce cling. The pasta is now
ready to be mixed with the sauce
of your choice.

Evan Kleiman created this recipe to debunk the myth that
good Italian cooking is heavy and take hours to prepare. The
sauce is uncooked. You can set the tomato mixture aside to
marinate in the morning before going to work. When you
come home all you need to do is prepare the spaghetti and
toss it with the tomatoes and cheese.

Make this dish in the summertime when the sweetest tomatoes and fresh basil are available. Evan suggests a quick
dinner of Spaghetti *alla Checca*, crusty bread, a garden salad
and a bottle of Chianti.

5 ripe tomatoes, stems removed and cut in ½-inch dice
2 garlic cloves, finely diced
6 leaves fresh basil, roughly chopped
salt to taste
1 cup virgin olive oil
8 ounces fresh mozzarella in water, cut in ¼-inch dice
1 pound spaghetti
freshly grated Parmesan cheese

1. In a small bowl, combine the tomatoes, garlic, basil and
salt to taste. Add only enough olive oil to just cover the tomato
mixture. Let marinate at room temperature for a minimum of
2 hours or up to 8 hours or so.

2. When you begin to prepare the spaghetti, take the diced
mozzarella out of the refrigerator and drain it of water.

3. Cook the spaghetti in a large quantity of rapidly boiling
salted water, until *al dente*, about 8 minutes. Drain and, in a
large bowl, immediately mix the tomato mixture and cheese
with the spaghetti. Serve immediately with freshly grated Parmesan cheese.

Serves 4 to 6

Spaghetti Cacio Pepe

Antonio Orlando of Valentino

Antonio tailored this exceptionally spicy, rich pasta dish to American tastes. Surprisingly, he finds that Americans prefer more spice in their food, especially more garlic and onion, than Italians do.

The *cacio pepe* cheese, which melts beautifully, can be found in Italian markets. It's a semi-hard sheep's milk cheese studded with whole black peppercorns. Swiss cheese or Asiago can be substituted if you add a teaspoon of cracked black peppercorns. Antonio suggests whole wheat pasta as an excellent vehicle for the hearty sauce.

1 tablespoon unsalted butter
½ cup chopped onion
½ cup heavy cream
1 teaspoon black olive puree or paste (available at Italian markets)
1 teaspoon freshly ground black pepper
½ teaspoon dry red chile flakes (optional)
½ pound cacio pepe *cheese, freshly grated*
1 pound spaghetti

1. Melt the butter in a 10-inch sauté pan. Add the onions and sauté over medium heat until soft, about 5 minutes.

2. Add the cream, olive puree, pepper and chile flakes, if desired. Bring to a boil and cook for 1 minute, stirring occasionally. Remove from heat and whisk in half the cheese.

3. Cook the pasta in a large quantity of rapidly boiling, salted water until *al dente*, about 8 minutes. (See page 34 for tips on cooking pasta.) Drain thoroughly and add to the sauce in the pan. Toss to coat the pasta. Add the remaining cheese; toss and serve immediately.

Serves 6

Grating Hard Cheeses

If possible buy hard cheeses such as Parmesan, Romano and Asiago in bulk and grate as needed. The result will be much more flavorful. Bring the cheese to room temperature and make sure you can get the tip of a sharp knife into it. Cut into one-inch cubes and grate in a processor fitted with a metal blade until fine.

Bow Tie Pasta in Salmon Sauce

Celestino Drago of Celestino's

Celestino started working in restaurants when he was in school and quickly learned that he loved the kitchen. By the time he was eighteen, he was head chef at one of the best restaurants in Tuscany, where this traditional pasta dish was served. The rich, creamy sauce also goes well with fettuccine or linguine. Celestino suggests serving this dish with a simple grilled meat entrée or with a salad as an impressive main-course pasta.

8 tablespoons (1 stick) unsalted butter
5 ounces smoked salmon, finely chopped
1 small shallot, minced
1 tablespoon brandy
1 pint (2 cups) heavy cream
1 pound farfalle or bow tie pasta
4 egg yolks, beaten
1 tablespoon fresh chives, minced, or 1 teaspoon dried
salt and freshly ground pepper to taste

1. Melt the butter in a medium-sized skillet over medium heat. Sauté the salmon and shallots about 2 minutes, until the shallots are soft.

2. Add the brandy and ignite it with a match. When the flame subsides add cream. Cook over medium-high heat until the liquid is reduced by half.

3. While the sauce is reducing, cook the pasta in a large quantity of rapidly boiling salted water until *al dente*, about 10 minutes. Drain in a colander. See page 34 for tips on cooking pasta.

4. Transfer the pasta to a large bowl. Pour in the cream mixture, egg yolks and chives. Mix well to coat the pasta; add salt and pepper to taste and serve immediately.

Serves 6 as an appetizer
    4 as an entrée

Pasta Jardinière

Cecilia De Castro of Ma Cuisine

This healthy pasta and vegetable dish is an easy weeknight dinner. It takes about fifteen minutes to prepare and the tastes are light, fresh and satisfying. You can substitute fresh vegetables or herbs of your choice.

2 carrots, peeled and cut in 2-inch julienne strips
1 zucchini, cored and julienned
1 leek, white part only, sliced in half lengthwise and julienned
1 pound linguine
2 tablespoons unsalted butter
1½ tablespoons heavy cream
2 tablespoons fresh tarragon, chopped
2 tablespoons fresh basil, chopped
salt and freshly ground pepper to taste
1 cup grated Parmesan cheese

1. Blanch the carrots in rapidly boiling water for 2 minutes. Refresh immediately in cold water. Repeat the procedure with zucchini for 2 minutes and leek for 3 minutes. Pat the vegetables dry.

2. Cook the pasta in a large quantity of rapidly boiling water until *al dente*, about 8 minutes. Drain and set aside. (See page 34 for tips on cooking pasta.)

3. Melt the butter in a 10-inch sauté pan over medium-high heat. Sauté the vegetables until just crisp, about 2 minutes. Add the cream and bring the mixture to a boil. Remove from heat. Add the tarragon, basil, salt and pepper and then the pasta. Toss until the pasta is well coated. Sprinkle with ½ cup of Parmesan, toss again and serve with the remaining Parmesan.

Serves 6

How to Clean and Chop a Leek

Leeks are a mild-tasting member of the onion family. Their long, many-layered leaves tend to collect soil, so it is important to clean them well before cooking. Trim the roots and green leaves and discard. Slice the leek in half lengthwise and rinse under cold, running water, separating the layers with your fingers to remove any grit. Place on the counter, cut side down, and slice lengthwise into quarter-inch strips.

Fettuccine Chicken Tequila

Ed La Dou of Caioti

Tequila

Tequila is a liquor distilled from
the heart of the Agave tequilana
plant. It is named for the small
town of Tequila in the state of
Jalisco where the best tequila is
said to be made.

Tequila is available in three
types: white, which is best for
mixed drinks like Margaritas; pale
gold, which is aged for a year and
is suitable for cooking and for
drinking alone, and the paler gold
añejo, which is the oldest and
most costly and which should be
savored straight.

Ed combines two of his favorite cuisines—Mexican and Italian—in this colorful pasta dish. The spicy Mexican flavors of *jalapeño* peppers and *cilantro* are balanced by the mild pasta. Tequila, rather than wine, adds a Mexican touch to the creamy sauce. This is a beautiful dish to serve at a casual dinner or lunch with a bottle of robust Chianti or Zinfandel.

1 jalapeño *pepper*
1 *whole chicken breast, skinless and boneless*
½ *cup chicken stock (page 224) or canned chicken broth*
2 *tablespoons unsalted butter*
1 *red bell pepper, cored, seeded and julienned*
1 *yellow bell pepper, cored, seeded and julienned*
1 *green bell pepper, cored, seeded and julienned*
½ *red onion, thinly sliced*
2 *ounces tequila*
4 *tablespoons fresh* cilantro, *or Chinese parsley, stems removed and chopped*
1 *pound spinach fettuccine*
1 *cup heavy cream*
juice of 1 lime
salt and freshly ground pepper to taste

1. Roast the *jalapeño* over a gas flame or under an electric broiler until the skin blackens. Carefully remove the skin following the procedure for roasting peppers on page 14. Split open the *jalapeño* and remove the seeds and ribs. Slice in fine julienne and reserve.

2. Slice the chicken in ¼-inch strips.

3. In a small saucepan, boil the chicken stock until it's reduced by half. Reserve.

4. While the stock is reducing cook the fettuccine in a large quantity of rapidly boiling salted water until *al dente,* about 8 minutes. (See page 34 for tips on cooking pasta.)

5. Melt the butter in a 10-inch sauté pan. Sauté the *jalapeño,* chicken, bell peppers and onion over medium-high heat until the chicken is opaque, about 2 to 3 minutes.

6. Add half the tequila and continue to cook for 2 minutes.

7. Add the reduced chicken stock and *cilantro.* Cook until the liquid in the pan is reduced by half.

8. Pour in the cream, turn the heat to high and cook until the sauce thickens, about 3 minutes.

9. Add the lime juice and season to taste with salt and pepper.

10. When pasta is ready, drain in a colander. Transfer to the sauté pan and toss with the warm sauce. Serve immediately.

Serves 4

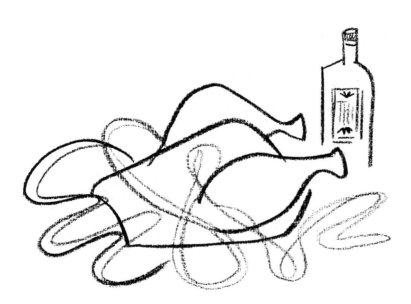

Lasagne Pesto

Antonio Orlando of Valentino

In this meatless lasagne, Antonio combines a favorite Italian sauce—*pesto*—with one of America's favorite pastas—lasagne—for an unusually elegant vegetarian main course.

Pesto and béchamel can be put to many other uses. The *pesto*, which keeps in the refrigerator for about a week, is wonderful with pasta or soup, or on steamed fish. Béchamel, which can also be refrigerated, is a classic component of soufflés and other sauces.

¾ pound spinach lasagne noodles
salt

Cook the noodles in 4 quarts of rapidly boiling, salted water until *al dente*. Rinse with cold water and set aside in a bowl of cool water. (See page 34 for tips on cooking pasta.)

PESTO SAUCE

2 garlic cloves
2 bunches basil, stems removed
½ cup pine nuts, toasted
½ cup grated Parmesan cheese
1 cup extra virgin olive oil
½ teaspoon salt

To make the *pesto:* In a food processor or a blender, mince the garlic. Add basil, nuts and Parmesan. Process until fine, about 1 minute. Keep the machine running and pour in the oil in a slow, steady stream. Add salt and pepper, process briefly and reserve.

BÉCHAMEL SAUCE

4 cups milk
1 slice of onion
1 bay leaf
8 tablespoons (1 stick) unsalted butter
½ cup all-purpose flour
½ teaspoon salt
¼ teaspoon white pepper
¼ teaspoon freshly grated nutmeg
2 pounds part-skim ricotta cheese
1 cup grated Parmesan cheese

1. To make the béchamel: Combine the milk, onion and bay leaf in a large saucepan. Bring to a boil and set aside to cool. In another large saucepan, melt the butter over low heat. Add the flour, whisking constantly, until the color turns blond, about 5 minutes. Gradually whisk in the warm milk, after discarding the bay leaf and onion. Cook over low heat until the mixture returns to a boil, whisking constantly. Remove from the heat. Whisk in the salt, pepper and nutmeg; reserve.

2. Preheat oven to 350°F.

3. In a large mixing bowl combine the ricotta, all the *pesto* and ¾ of the béchamel. Taste and adjust the seasonings.

4. Drain the pasta and pat dry with paper towels.

5. To assemble the lasagne: Lightly oil a 9 × 13-inch baking dish. Arrange alternating layers of noodles and the ricotta mixture, beginning and ending with the noodles. Pour on the remaining béchamel and sprinkle the top with Parmesan.

6. Bake for 45 minutes, or until golden brown and bubbly. Let stand for 10 minutes before slicing and serving.

Serves 10 to 12

Béchamel

Béchamel—it has traditionally been called white sauce in America—is one of the basic, or mother, sauces of classic French cooking. The butter and flour mixture that thickens the sauce is called a *roux*. Be careful not to overcook the *roux*. If you do, it will turn brown, as in Cajun cooking. Keep the heat very low and whisk constantly. The mixture should become a very pale yellow and lose the starchy taste of the flour.

Béchamel is the base for Mornay sauce, with grated Parmesan or Gruyère, Nantua, with shrimp butter and cream, and Florentine, with chopped spinach and nutmeg. The base for hot soufflés is a combination of béchamel, egg yolks and flavorings such as cheese or spinach.

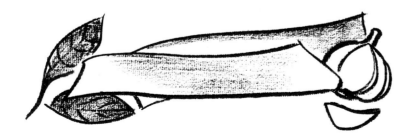

Pansotti with Walnut Sauce

Antonio Orlando of Valentino

The recipe for this extremely rich pasta was given to Antonio by a friend's grandmother in Liguria. The *pansotti*, which are large-size ravioli, are stuffed with a smooth mixture of spinach and ricotta and then generously coated with the creamy walnut sauce. One taste will tell you why this is one of the most popular dishes at Valentino.

The chef suggests following this luxurious pasta with a simply prepared grilled steak or fish entrée. Piero Selvaggio, the restaurant's owner and wine specialist, recommends a crisp, well-balanced red wine such as Vino Nobile to complement the full flavors.

FILLING

1 pound part-skim ricotta cheese
*2 (10-ounce) packages frozen chopped spinach, cooked briefly
  and drained*
2 eggs
¾ cup grated Parmesan cheese
2 teaspoons salt
1½ teaspoons freshly grated nutmeg
¼ teaspoon freshly ground pepper

Combine all the filling ingredients in a large bowl and reserve.

PASTA

1 recipe Egg Pasta dough (page 229)
1 egg, lightly beaten

1. Knead and stretch the dough (page 229) and cut it into 12-inch lengths.
2. To stuff the pasta: Place a sheet of pasta dough on a floured countertop. Brush lightly with the egg. Place a teaspoon of filling every 1½ inches, forming two rows of filling.

3. Top with another sheet of pasta. Press down to seal the pasta around the filling and remove the air. With a pastry wheel, cut between the piles of filling to make 2-inch squares. The *pansotti* can be made in advance and placed on floured or oiled baking sheets for several hours. To freeze, set aside to dry and then seal in plastic freezer bags.

WALNUT SAUCE

2 garlic cloves
2½ cups walnut halves
1 cup pine nuts
3 cups heavy cream
3 tablespoons unsalted butter, room temperature
2 tablespoons olive oil

1. To make the sauce: In a food processor fitted with a metal blade, mince the garlic. Add the nuts and process until very fine. With the machine running, gradually pour in 2 cups of the cream, 2 tablespoons of the butter and all the oil. Process another 30 seconds and reserve.

2. Combine the remaining tablespoon of butter and cup of cream in a medium-sized skillet. Cook over high heat until the cream is reduced by half. Reduce the heat to low and whisk in the pureed nut mixture.

3. While the cream is reducing, cook the *pansotti* in 4 quarts of rapidly boiling salted water for about 3 minutes. Drain.

4. Transfer the pasta to the warm sauce in the skillet. Toss to coat. Place on serving dishes and serve immediately with freshly grated Parmesan cheese.

Serves 8

Cooking with Fresh Pasta

Fresh pasta can be made several hours before cooking. Reserve the pasta on flour-lined baking trays and cover them with plastic wrap. Long noodles like spaghetti should be wound into small nests, and stuffed pasta like ravioli should lay in a single layer.

As when cooking dry pasta, fresh pasta should be cooked in a large pot with a minimum of three quarts of water and one tablespoon salt. Bring the water to a rapid boil, add the pasta and stir occasionally to prevent sticking. It's important not to reduce the heat, but always keep it at a rapid boil. Fresh pasta cooks much faster than dry; about one minute for long noodles and two or three minutes for stuffed. Taste it and, as soon as the pasta is *al dente* (firm, not soft, to the bite), drain. Do not rinse unless you're using for a cold pasta salad or you need to handle it, as for lasagne.

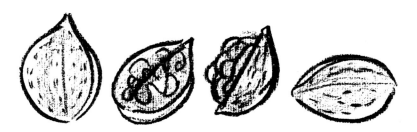

Red Pepper Pasta with Grilled Lobster*

Michael McCarty of Michael's

Opening his own restaurant enabled Michael to combine his passion for throwing a great party with the knowledge of food and restaurants he gained while studying at the Cordon Bleu in Paris and at hotel schools both in Paris and New York.

His goal at the restaurant has always been to serve the very best ingredients in the most simple and correct way. He favors luxurious ingredients like lobster but prefers serving them informally, as in this dish of grilled lobster over a bed of red pepper pasta in classic lobster sauce. If pasta making is not your cup of tea, substitute 1 pound of thin commercial pasta such as spaghettini or angel hair. Or, if your store carries it, a tomato-flavored pasta will supply the color.

RED PEPPER PASTA

3 red bell peppers, roasted, peeled and seeded (page 14)
3 egg yolks
4 to 4½ cups all-purpose flour

1. In a food processor, combine the red peppers, egg yolks and flour. Process until the dough forms small beads that clump together. Press the dough into a ball. Wrap in plastic wrap and set aside to rest at room temperature for about 15 minutes.

2. Cut the dough into four equal pieces; rewrap three in plastic and start kneading the fourth ball of dough with the pasta machine at the widest setting. Flatten the dough by hand and roll it through once. Fold the dough in half and roll it again, and repeat ten times, until the dough is perfectly smooth.

3. To stretch the dough, with the machine at the next widest setting roll the dough through twice. Reduce the setting, rolling the dough through twice at each setting until you reach the next to the last setting. Lay the completed dough on a lightly floured counter and repeat the entire procedure with the remaining three pieces of dough.

*From *Michael's Cookbook* by Michael McCarty.

4. When the stretching process is completed, cut the dough very fine, into angel hair, and lay the finished pasta in nests on floured counters to dry, about 10 minutes. For complete pasta-making instructions see Egg Pasta (page 229).

LOBSTER SAUCE

2 (1½-pound) lobsters
2 cups dry, white wine
4 shallots, minced
½ bunch fresh parsley
5 sprigs thyme
1 bay leaf
3 black peppercorns
2 cups heavy cream

1. Bring a large stockpot of water to a boil. Add the lobsters and cook 5 minutes. Rinse in cold water until the lobster is cool enough to handle. Remove the meat and reserve the shells. Leave the claw meat whole and slice the tails into ¾-inch slices. Reserve.

2. Combine the lobster shells, wine, shallots, parsley, thyme, bay leaf and peppercorns in a medium saucepan. Add enough water to cover and bring to a boil. Reduce the heat and cook over medium heat for 20 minutes.

3. Pass the mixture through a strainer, draining into a large sauté pan. Cook the liquid over high heat until it is reduced to about ½ cup. This will take about 20 minutes.

4. Pour in the cream and boil briskly until sauce is thick enough to coat a spoon, about 10 minutes. Keep warm over very low heat while preparing the pasta and lobster.

GRILLED LOBSTER

reserved lobster meat
2 tablespoons unsalted butter, melted
salt and freshly ground pepper to taste
1 bunch fresh basil, stems removed and julienned (garnish)

1. Preheat the grill or broiler.

How Much Flour to Use to Make Pasta

Because the humidity in the air and the moisture the flour has already absorbed in storage vary so, it's hard to specify exactly how much flour to use. The best way to gauge is to start with the lower quantity listed in the recipe, start processing and stop processing frequently to check the dough's consistency. Perfect pasta dough should hold together when the morsels are pressed, without being sticky or dry. Sticky dough needs more flour.

2. Bring a large sauce pan of salted water to a boil.

3. Brush the reserved lobster meat with melted butter and season lightly with salt and pepper. Grill or broil about ½ minute per side.

4. Add the pasta to the boiling water and cook until *al dente*, ½ to 1 minute if fresh, about 8 minutes if using prepared pasta. Drain and transfer the pasta to the warm sauce. Toss to coat.

5. To serve: Divide the pasta among six serving plates. Divide the lobster meat and place on top of each serving. Garnish with basil and serve immediately.

Serves 6

Basmati Rice

Susan Feniger and Mary Sue Milliken of City Restaurant

Basmati rice adds an authentic Indian touch to the Spicy City Chicken on page 105 and to curries and stir-fry dishes. Grown at the base of the Himalayas, this rice is prized in India for its aromatic flavor and unusually thin, toothy grain. It's available at gourmet, health food and Indian markets.

2 cups basmati *rice*
3½ cups water
⅛ teaspoon salt
4 tablespoons (½ stick) unsalted butter, room temperature

1. Rinse the rice in cold water until the water runs clear. Drain.

2. Bring the water to a boil in a medium-sized saucepan with a tight-fitting lid. Add the salt and rice; return to a boil. Reduce heat to medium and cook for 6 minutes, covered.

3. Remove from heat and let stand, covered, for 10 minutes. Add the butter and toss to coat the rice. Serve immediately with Spicy City Chicken or your favorite stir-fry dish.

Serves 6 to 8

How to Rinse Rice

Rinsing removes the excess starch and gives all rice, not just *basmati*, cleaner flavor. Place the uncooked rice in a large mixing bowl; fill with cold water and stir by hand until the water turns milky. Pour off the water and repeat this procedure twice for a purer, nuttier-tasting rice.

Mon Kee Fried Rice

Michael Kojima of Mon Kee

Restaurant quality fried rice is surprisingly easy to make. The key is chilling the cooked white rice before stir-frying. This fried rice is substantial enough to serve as a main course for a light supper or with any barbecued meat, chicken or fish. Vary the amount of shrimp, pork or ham in the rice to your taste. You can also add small chunks of cooked beef or chicken, if desired.

4 tablespoons oil, peanut or soybean
4 ounces shrimp, shelled, deveined and split in half
4 ounces cooked pork, cut in 1/4-inch cubes
4 ounces honey-cured ham, cut in 1/4-inch cubes
2 eggs, beaten
3 1/2 cups cooked white rice, cold
3 scallions, white and green parts, minced
2 teaspoons soy sauce
freshly ground pepper

1. Heat wok over high heat. Swirl in 2 tablespoons of the oil to coat. Add shrimp and stir-fry for 30 seconds. Add pork and stir-fry an additional 2 minutes and add ham for another 30 seconds. Remove and reserve the stir-fried ingredients.

2. Add the eggs and stir gently to scramble. Do not overcook. The eggs should remain soft and runny. Remove and reserve. Wipe the wok clean with paper towels, being careful not to burn yourself.

3. Swirl in the remaining 2 tablespoons oil. Add the rice and stir-fry for 2 to 3 minutes, separating the grains.

4. Return the shrimp, pork, ham and egg to the wok. Add the scallions and soy sauce. Stir-fry briefly until the combination is well mixed and the egg is broken into small pieces. Season with pepper and serve immediately.

Serves 4 to 6

Rice in China

Rice is the focus of the meal in southern China, while noodles and other wheat-based products are more popular in the north. Unlike the American style of eating rice as an accompaniment to more elaborate dishes, in China rice is the main course, served with side dishes. The Chinese prefer their rice cooked without butter or salt to change the flavor. In China, fried rice is eaten as a snack or small meal but never in place of white rice.

Risotto Verde

Celestino Drago of Celestino's

Sweet peas and spinach add a dash of color to this classic Italian rice dish. Celestino suggests serving it when the weather is cool and you're not in a rush, since the rice needs constant attention for about 20 minutes. Put on some good music, get ready to stir and enjoy this delectably creamy rice.

5 tablespoons unsalted butter
2 small leeks, white part only, finely chopped
2 cups Arborio rice (available at Italian markets)
½ cup dry white wine
1 cup fresh sweet peas
4 cups chicken stock (page 224) or canned chicken broth, warm
1 pound spinach, stems removed
½ cup grated Parmesan cheese
salt and freshly ground pepper to taste

1. Melt 1 tablespoon of the butter in a large saucepan. Over medium heat, sauté the leeks about 3 minutes until golden brown. Add rice and wine and cook until the wine evaporates, stirring occasionally. Stir in the peas.

2. Start adding the chicken stock, 1 cup at a time, stirring constantly after each addition. After each cup has been absorbed, add the next, until about 3½ cups are absorbed. The rice must be stirred constantly.

3. While the rice is cooking, bring the remaining ½ cup of stock to a boil in a small pan. Add the spinach and cook until it wilts, about 5 minutes.

4. Transfer the spinach and stock to the rice and cook until all the stock is absorbed.

5. Remove from heat and stir in the remaining butter and Parmesan cheese until melted. Add salt and pepper to taste, mix well and serve immediately.

Serves 6

Cooking Risotto

There is no substitute for Arborio rice when cooking *risotto*. This short round grain from northern Italy is much more absorbent than other varieties of rice. Risotto is always cooked uncovered and must be stirred constantly. It takes some practice to learn the right moment to add each cup of broth. Although the previous cup of broth should be absorbed, the rice grains should be slightly moist rather than totally dry. Stir in the butter and Parmesan cheese *off* the heat and serve immediately, so the grains don't stick together.

BREAD & PIZZA

Ed La Dou's Pizza Dough

Great Pizza

Before you look at individual recipes, you should know that the key to making great pizza is organization. Make sure all your toppings are ready before you start rolling out the dough. The oven should be preheated at the highest setting, with the cooking surface (stone, tiles or cookie sheet) placed inside. Have platters and a spatula ready nearby for quick pizza removal, since a minute or two extra can make the difference between a perfect crust and a burnt one.

It takes time and some practice to make pizza dough from scratch, especially if you haven't worked with a yeast dough before, but the results are incomparable. We suggest making the whole recipe, enough for six individual pizzas, and storing any leftover dough in the freezer for impromptu gatherings. Just form the dough into balls and wrap with two layers of plastic wrap. They'll keep in the freezer indefinitely, but remember to allow enough time for the dough to return to room temperature before rolling it out. Since it takes about an hour for the preparation and rising, leave plenty of time before serving.

1 package (1 tablespoon) dry yeast
1 1/2 tablespoons granulated sugar
1 1/2 cups warm water
3 1/2 cups all-purpose flour
1/2 cup semolina
1 tablespoon salt
3 tablespoons olive oil

KNEADING BY HAND

1. Dissolve the yeast and sugar in 1/2 cup of the warm water. Let stand until foamy, about 10 minutes.

2. Combine the flour, semolina and salt in a large mixing bowl.

3. Add the olive oil and stir with a wooden spoon until the oil is absorbed.

4. Stir in the yeast mixture and then gradually stir in the remaining water until the dough is stiff and a little sticky.

5. Turn the dough onto a very lightly floured board. Knead until smooth and elastic, about 7 minutes. After kneading, the dough should be firm and moist.

6. Cover with a damp towel and set aside to rest about 20 minutes.

7. For individual pizzas, divide the dough into 6 equal pieces. Form each portion into a ball by briefly kneading and then folding the edges up and tucking them into the center.

About Semolina

Semolina is a coarse flour derived from hard durum wheat. Its mealy consistency and high gluten content give pizza its chewiness. If it is not available at your supermarket, try an Italian specialty market. Semolina is a basic ingredient of Italian pasta and bread making. Farina may be substituted for semolina, but make sure it's not the fast-cooking breakfast variety.

Cover the balls with a damp towel and set aside to rest about 45 minutes, or until they increase about 20 percent in size. They can now be rolled out for pizza making or wrapped in plastic wrap and stored in the refrigerator or freezer.

KNEADING WITH THE FOOD PROCESSOR

Although Ed La Dou swears by the hand method for the most authentic pizza crust, Ma Cuisine has developed a food processor method that reduces preparation time dramatically. We recommend you make your first batch of dough by hand, to experience what properly kneaded dough feels like. If you do, you'll stand a better chance of judging the exact moment to stop processing.

1. Dissolve the yeast and sugar in ½ cup warm water and let stand until foamy, about 10 minutes.

2. In a food processor fitted with a plastic dough blade, combine flour, semolina and salt. Add the oil and process about 30 seconds to combine.

3. With the machine running, add the yeast mixture. Gradually add the remaining 1 cup of water in a slow, steady stream until the dough clears the sides of the workbowl. When the dough forms a ball around the blade, enough water has been added. Process an additional minute.

4. Remove the dough from the workbowl and shape into a ball. Follow the same procedure as steps 6 and 7 of the hand method for proper rising.

Yields 6 individual pizzas

Pizza Tips from Ed La Dou

When creating your own combinations, Ed suggests you think of pizza as you would another starch-plus-topping combination—the sandwich. Whatever tastes good on a sandwich would probably make a good pizza.

- Limit yourself to three to five toppings at the beginning.
- Start with a main ingredient, either meat or vegetable, a vegetable accompaniment, an herb, and a cheese to melt and carry the flavors.
- Always coat the dough with a layer of sauce or oil before you start assembling the pizza so the toppings don't stick.
- Remember to leave about an inch bare around the edges to form the crust.
- Spread the ingredients consistently so that, ideally, any single bite contains all of the flavors.

Pizza Puttanesca
Ed La Dou of Caioti

For those who like pizza Italian-style, *puttanesca* combines the traditional tomato sauce and mozzarella cheese with the spicy tastes of garlic, prosciutto, olives and capers. The tomato sauce is uncooked and can be combined in a few minutes. (See the note for baking pizza.)

TOMATO SAUCE

10 Italian plum tomatoes, peeled, seeded and coarsely chopped
12 fresh basil leaves, chopped
4 tablespoons tomato paste
1 teaspoon salt
1 teaspoon white pepper
¼ teaspoon cayenne

Combine the sauce ingredients in a bowl and reserve.

12 garlic cloves, peeled
4 (5-ounce) pizza dough balls (page 50)
⅓ cup Kalamata olives, pitted and halved
6 ounces prosciutto, thinly sliced
1 pound mozzarella cheese, grated
3 tablespoons capers
1 tablespoon fresh oregano, chopped, or 1 teaspoon dried

1. Blanch the garlic in simmering water for 3 minutes. Rinse with cold water and reserve.

2. Preheat oven to 500°F.

3. On a very lightly floured surface, roll out each dough ball to form an 8-inch wide circle.

4. To assemble: Leaving a one-inch edge for the crust, place a quarter of the sauce in the center of each pizza and spread to cover the dough. Sprinkle with olives. Arrange the prosciutto over the olives. Sprinkle each with ½ cup mozzarella. Top with garlic cloves, capers and oregano, if using dried.

5. Bake for 6 to 10 minutes or until the crust is golden and the cheese is bubbly. Sprinkle with fresh oregano and serve immediately.

Yields four 8-inch pizzas

Barbecued Chicken Pizza

Ed La Dou of Caioti

It's hard to imagine a more unlikely or more delicious combination than this barbecued chicken pizza with smoked Gouda cheese and sweet red onion. It is the most popular item at California Pizza Kitchen, whose menu Ed designed. There's no precooking involved. The chicken is marinated, but it is cooked along with the pizza.

1 chicken breast, skinless and boneless
4 (5-ounce) pizza dough balls (page 50)
8 ounces prepared barbecue sauce, smoky preferred
1 pound mozzarella cheese, grated
8 ounces smoked Gouda cheese, grated
4 tablespoons fresh cilantro, *or Chinese parsley, stems removed and chopped*
1 small red onion, thinly sliced

1. Slice the chicken into ¼-inch strips. Marinate in barbecue sauce for about 1 hour, at room temperature.
2. Preheat the oven to 500°F.
3. On a lightly floured surface, roll out each dough ball to form an 8-inch wide circle.
4. To assemble: Leaving a one-inch edge for the crust, brush each circle with 1 tablespoon of the marinade. Divide the Gouda cheese and half of the mozzarella into four portions. Spread the cheese evenly on top of the sauce. Divide and arrange the chicken slices over the cheese. Sprinkle generously with *cilantro*. Top with onion slices and sprinkle with the remaining mozzarella cheese.
5. Bake for 6 to 10 minutes or until the crust is golden and the cheese is bubbly. Serve immediately.

Yields four 8-inch pizzas

Participation Pizza Party

Pizza is the perfect party food because it's a one-dish meal that can be eaten by hand. Everybody likes It and, best of all, you can get your guests to help make it. All you need is a refrigerator full of cold drinks, a large green salad, plenty of napkins and steady nerves.

Spread a buffet table with assorted shredded cheeses, chopped vegetables and herbs, marinated bits of meat, and a few easy sauces and olive oil. Pass the rolling pin and watch your guests design their own California pizzas.

Thai Shrimp Pizza

Ed La Dou of Caioti

When Wolfgang Puck hired Ed to be the first pizza chef at Spago, his only request was that he make the best pizza in America. With a wide variety of fresh ingredients at his disposal Ed created individual pizzas without roots in Italian or Mediterranean cuisine. This Thai pizza, among Spago's most popular, is typical of his inventiveness. It takes a bit longer to prepare than the others because the shrimp are marinated for an hour and the vegetables sautéed, but the results are worth it.

4 (5-ounce) pizza dough balls (page 50)
¼ cup olive oil
1 teaspoon crushed red chiles
10 large shrimp, peeled, deveined and split lengthwise
1 large zucchini, seeded and julienned
½ red or yellow bell pepper, cored, seeded and julienned
8 ounces mozzarella cheese, grated
2 ounces fontina cheese, grated
1 large tomato, peeled, seeded and chopped (page 19)
1 tablespoon fresh mint, stems removed and chopped
¼ red onion, thinly sliced
juice of 1 lime

   1. Preheat oven to 500°F.

   2. Combine the olive oil and chiles in a small bowl. Add the shrimp and set aside to marinate for an hour at room temperature.

   3. When the shrimp are finished marinating, transfer them to a small bowl, reserving the marinade.

4. In a small skillet, heat 1 tablespoon of the oil and chile mixture over low heat. Sauté the zucchini and bell pepper until slightly golden. Reserve.

5. On a lightly floured surface, roll out each dough ball to form an 8-inch wide circle.

6. To assemble: Leaving a one-inch edge for the crust, brush the dough with the marinade. Divide the cheese and spread evenly, reserving a couple of spoonfuls for sprinkling. Add the tomatoes, followed by the zucchini and peppers. Divide the shrimp and arrange evenly over the top. Sprinkle with the mint, onion and remaining cheese.

7. Bake for 6 to 10 minutes or until the crust is golden and the cheese is bubbly. Drizzle with lime juice and serve immediately.

Yields four 8-inch pizzas

Chile Cornbread Muffins

Leonard Schwartz of 72 Market Street

These spicy little muffins combine all the condiments of chili with the earthy texture of cornmeal. As with quickbreads, the combining can be done by hand with a wooden spoon. The batter should be *very* lumpy. These muffins are served alongside Kick-Ass Chili (page 115) at the restaurant, and would go well with assorted omelets at brunch.

2 tablespoons rendered bacon fat or softened butter
1 ¼ cups all-purpose flour
1 cup yellow cornmeal
1 ½ tablespoons baking powder
1 ½ tablespoons cumin
½ tablespoon salt
½ tablespoon crushed red chile flakes
1 cup milk
1 ½ cups sour cream
2 medium eggs
4 tablespoons unsalted butter, melted
½ pound sharp cheddar cheese, grated
3 poblano or pasilla chiles, seeded and minced
4 scallions, white and green parts, minced
1 (12-ounce) can corn

1. Preheat oven to 350°F. Grease two muffin tins with the rendered bacon fat or butter and set aside.

2. Combine the flour, cornmeal, baking powder, cumin, salt and chile flakes in a large mixing bowl.

3. In another mixing bowl, combine the milk, sour cream, eggs and butter.

4. Stir the dry ingredients into the liquid until just combined.

5. Stir in the cheese, chiles, scallions and corn until combined. The batter will be quite thick and lumpy.

6. Spoon ½ cup batter into each muffin cup. Bake for 20 to 25 minutes, until a cake tester inserted in the center comes out clean. Set aside to cool in the tin for about 10 minutes and serve warm.

Yields 18 muffins

Chocolate Orange Brioches

Renée Carisio of Ma Cuisine

Store-bought *brioches* pale by comparison with these rich, golden cakes, flecked with orange peel and huge chunks of dark chocolate. Plan ahead, because the dough needs to rise three times—including once in the refrigerator overnight—to achieve the proper consistency.

½ cup milk
½ cup granulated sugar
2 packages yeast
zest of 2 oranges
2 eggs
4 egg yolks
3 cups all-purpose flour
2 teaspoons salt
1 cup (2 sticks) + 1 tablespoon unsalted butter, cold
6 ounces bittersweet chocolate, roughly chopped

No Need to Knead

The few minutes that the dough is mixed in the electric mixer provide all the kneading required for light, cakey *brioches*. Because you want to inhibit gluten, which gives bread its chewiness, classic *brioche* dough is allowed to rise slowly over a long period of time, with no kneading.

1. Scald the milk and let it cool to 110°F. Add ¼ cup of the sugar and the yeast and let stand until foamy, about 10 minutes. (See page 64 for proofing yeast.)

2. Combine the orange zest with the remaining sugar in a food processor and process until zest is finely ground.

3. In a heavy-duty electric mixer, combine the yeast mixture, zest and sugar mixture, eggs and egg yolks. Beat until combined, about 30 seconds.

4. In a separate bowl, sift together the flour and salt. Gradually add the dry ingredients to the liquid in the mixer bowl, beating constantly until the dough is sticky and soft.

5. Add 2 sticks of butter, 1 tablespoon at a time, beating constantly until combined. Beat an additional 30 seconds.

6. Coat a large bowl with the remaining tablespoon of butter. Turn the dough out onto a lightly floured board; form a ball *without kneading* and place in the bowl, turning to coat the dough with butter. Cover with plastic wrap and a towel and set aside to rise in a warm place until doubled in bulk, about 1 to 1½ hours.

7. Turn the dough out onto a lightly floured board. Punch down to remove air bubbles and return to the bowl. Cover

with plastic wrap and refrigerate a minimum of 6 hours, or overnight.

8. Turn the dough out onto a lightly floured board and gently knead in the chocolate pieces. Divide the dough into 16 equal parts. Roll each between your hands to form a 1½-inch round cylinder. To make the traditional *brioche* topknot, lay the cylinders on a counter and roll the side of your hand back and forth at a point about an inch from the top, so you form a shape like a bowling pin. Place the dough in buttered *brioche* tins or muffin cups, pinched side up, and gently press the tops down toward the bottom of the tin.

9. Place the tins on a baking sheet, cover with plastic wrap and a towel and set aside in a warm place to rise until doubled, about 1½ hours.

10. Preheat oven to 375°F.

11. Bake for 20 minutes. While the *brioches* are baking, make the glaze.

ORANGE GLAZE

1 cup confectioners' sugar
3 tablespoons orange juice

Whisk the ingredients together to form a paste and spoon about 1 tablespoon over each warm *brioche*.

Yields 16 *brioches*

Chutney Bread with Curried Cream Cheese Spread

Michael Roberts of Trumps

Michael Roberts gives a classic quickbread recipe a distinctively British flavor with mango chutney. At the restaurant the bread is cut into small squares and the curried cream cheese (see next page) is piped through a star-tipped pastry bag.

You can adapt this recipe with your favorite fruit and nut combinations. Michael suggests ripe bananas and walnuts, blueberry chutney and pecans or sun-dried tomatoes and pine nuts. Have fun experimenting!

butter for coating pan
2 1/2 cups all-purpose flour
3 1/2 teaspoons baking powder
1 teaspoon salt
1 cup walnuts, coarsely chopped
1/2 cup granulated sugar
1/2 cup packed dark brown sugar
1 egg
1 1/4 cups milk
3 tablespoons vegetable oil
1 tablespoon grated orange zest
1 (10-ounce) jar mango chutney

1. Preheat oven to 350°F. Butter and flour a 9 × 5 × 3-inch loaf pan.

2. In a large mixing bowl stir the flour, baking powder, salt and nuts until combined.

3. In another bowl combine the sugars, egg, milk, oil, zest and chutney. All the mixing can be done by hand with a wooden spoon.

4. Add the dry ingredients to the liquid mixture and stir just until combined. The batter should be lumpy.

5. Pour the batter into the prepared pan. Bake for 1 hour and 15 minutes, or until a cake tester inserted in the center comes out clean.

6. Let the bread cool in the pan on a rack for 10 minutes. Remove from pan and cool on a rack until serving time.

Yields 1 loaf

The Secret of Successful Quickbreads

The key to baking tender fruit and nut breads is to work the ingredients by hand. All the combining can be done with a wooden spoon. Try to resist the temptation to overmix and develop the gluten. Remember, the lumpier the batter the more tender the quickbread or muffin.

CURRIED CREAM CHEESE SPREAD

8 ounces cream cheese, softened
½ cup confectioners' sugar
2 tablespoons curry powder

With an electric mixer or food processor, beat the cream
cheese until fluffy. Add the sugar and curry; beat until smooth
and serve on chutney bread.

Yields 1 cup

Currant-Walnut Baguettes

Renée Carisio of Ma Cuisine

This earthy brown bread, shaped into long thin *baguettes* and densely packed with raisins and walnuts, is virtually impossible to stop eating. Renée first tasted a similar bread at the two-starred Michel Rostang in Paris. She likes to serve it with hearty soups, such as cream of pumpkin or squash, with curried chicken salad or cream cheese spreads, and, of course, with fruit and cheese. Bread as good as this is worth the work.

1 package yeast
1½ tablespoons honey
1¼ cups warm water
1½ cups bread flour
1½ cups whole wheat flour
1 teaspoon salt
¾ cup walnut halves
¾ cup currants
¼ cup golden raisins
¼ cup raisins
butter for coating bowl
1 egg, beaten, for glaze

How to Guarantee a Crisp Crust

For a really crisp crust, you must add moisture to the loaf while it's baking. You can do this by placing a pan of water on a low rack in the oven, by spraying the bread with a plant mister two or three times while it's baking, or by baking the bread directly on a baker's stone that has been soaked in water. Any of these methods will result in a crisp crust.

1. Dissolve the yeast and honey in ¼ cup warm water and let stand until foamy, about 10 minutes. (See page 64 for proofing yeast.)

2. In a food processor fitted with a plastic dough blade, combine the flours and salt. Process about 30 seconds. Add the walnuts and process an additional 15 seconds. With the machine running, pour the yeast mixture through the feed tube.

3. With the machine running, slowly add 1 cup water through the feed tube. Process until the dough clears the sides of the bowl and is no longer dry, about 1 minute additional.

4. Turn out onto a lightly floured board and knead in the currants and raisins for about 5 minutes.

5. Coat a large bowl with butter. Transfer the dough to the bowl, turning to coat the top with butter. Cover with plastic wrap and a towel and set aside to rise in a warm place, until the dough is doubled in bulk, about 1 to 1½ hours.

6. Turn the dough out onto a lightly floured board. Punch down to remove air bubbles and divide the dough into two equal parts. Roll each part into a 6 x 15-inch sheet. Roll the sheets into long cylinders, pinching the edges to seal. Transfer the cylinders, seam side down, to a buttered baking sheet or two *baguette* pans. Cover with plastic wrap and a towel and set aside to rise until the dough is almost doubled, about 45 minutes.

7. Preheat oven to 425°F.

8. Brush the loaves with the beaten egg and slash each with a sharp knife several times along the diagonal. Bake for 30 to 40 minutes, until loaves are well browned.

Yields 2 loaves

Currant Scones

Michael Roberts of Trumps

When Michael Roberts and his partner opened Trumps, they decided to serve a late afternoon tea. Although it took a while for Angelenos to catch on, the old-fashioned idea of tea and sandwiches has made Trumps one of the most popular meeting places in town.

No tea would be complete without scones and these are not to be missed. Preparation time is about fifteen minutes in the food processor or with an electric mixer. Serve them warm with small pots of *crème fraîche* and your best preserves.

butter for coating pan
3 cups all-purpose flour
6 tablespoons granulated sugar
2 tablespoons plus 2 teaspoons baking powder
9 tablespoons (1 stick plus 1 tablespoon) unsalted butter, cold
1 cup currants
1 cup buttermilk, room temperature
1 egg, lightly beaten

1. Preheat oven to 325°F. Butter a large cookie sheet.
2. Combine flour, sugar and baking powder in a food processor. Process for about 30 seconds or mix just until blended.
3. Cut the butter into tablespoon-sized pieces and add to the dry ingredients. Combine with about 15 short pulses of the processor or until the mixture looks like a coarse meal. Mix in the currants until just combined.
4. With the processor or mixer running, pour in the buttermilk. Process until the batter looks crumbly and dry.
5. Turn the batter onto a lightly floured board. It's important when handling this dough to work it as little as possible. Press the dough together, forming a large ball. Divide it into three parts. Shape each into a circle 5 inches round by 1 inch thick. Place the circles on the prepared cookie sheet and score deeply—though not all the way through—in quarters.
6. Brush the tops with the beaten egg, being careful not to let the egg drip on the pan.
7. Bake for 25 minutes. The tops should be golden brown when done. Let cool for 10 minutes, pull apart and serve.

Yields 12 scones

How to Measure Dry Ingredients

Baking is a much more precise art than cooking and incorrect measuring can make the difference between success and failure in your baked goods.

First, *stir* the ingredients to be measured. *Scoop* them into the specified measuring cups without firmly packing. *Level* off the excess by sweeping the flat edge of a knife or spatula across the top.

Egg Bread

Renée Carisio of Ma Cuisine

Proofing Yeast

Occasionally, baking recipes will omit proofing the yeast as the first step. We recommend always taking the time to proof, before you begin baking, so that all the time you spend mixing and kneading is not wasted. Combine a quarter of whatever liquid the recipe calls for, warmed to 110° to 115°F, with the yeast and at least one tablespoon of the sweetener in the recipe. Set aside at room temperature until a layer of foam forms at the top. If there is no foam within ten minutes, discard and start again. Don't forget to check the expiration date. Dry yeast remains active only for about nine months.

Renée has been making this traditional American egg bread since her mother taught her how to bake, at age ten. The rich, eggy dough can be used for plain loaves, challah and a multitude of sweet roll variations. Two of Renée's favorites—Cinnamon Buns and Orange Pecan Rolls—follow.

2 packages yeast
¼ cup granulated sugar
¼ cup warm water
2 cups milk
4 tablespoons (½ stick) unsalted butter
2 teaspoons salt
2 eggs
5 to 5½ cups sifted all-purpose flour
butter for coating bowl

1. Dissolve the yeast and 1 tablespoon of the sugar in the warm water and let stand until foamy, about 10 minutes. (See note on this page for proofing yeast.)

2. Combine milk, butter, the remaining sugar and salt in a medium saucepan. Place over medium heat and cook until the butter melts. Set aside to cool to 110° to 115°F.

3. Combine the yeast mixture, warm milk mixture and eggs in the bowl of a heavy duty electric mixer. With the beaters on low speed, gradually add the flour, 1 cup at a time, until 3 cups have been added. Increase the speed to medium in order to smooth the dough, and then return to low speed. Gradually add the remaining flour until the dough is soft. Beat an additional 5 minutes to smooth out the dough. It should be very soft and sticky.

4. Turn out onto a *very* lightly floured board and knead for 2 to 3 minutes, until the dough is smooth and elastic.

5. Coat a large bowl with butter. Transfer the dough to the bowl, turning to coat the top with butter. Cover with plastic wrap and a towel and set aside to rise in a warm place until the dough is doubled in bulk, about 1 to 1½ hours.

CINNAMON BUNS

1 cup (2 sticks) for coating pans unsalted butter, softened
3 tablespoons granulated sugar
1 cup packed dark brown sugar
1 cup raisins
4 teaspoons cinnamon

1. While the dough is rising, prepare three 9-inch round cake pans. Coat each with 1 tablespoon butter and sprinkle with granulated sugar. Reserve.

2. Combine the brown sugar, raisins and cinnamon in a bowl and set aside.

3. When the dough is finished rising, turn out onto a lightly floured board. Punch down to remove air bubbles and divide the dough in two equal parts. Roll each into a 12 by 15-inch sheet. Spread each with 1 stick of butter and half the brown sugar mixture.

4. Roll the filled sheets into 15-inch long cylinders. Slice each into 1½-inch rounds and place in the prepared cake pans, with about 2 inches between the rolls so they have room to expand. Cover with plastic wrap and a towel and set aside to rise in a warm place for half an hour.

5. Preheat oven to 350°F.

6. Bake for 20 to 25 minutes. Invert onto serving platter and let cool slightly before serving.

Yields 14 to 18 buns

ORANGE PECAN ROLLS

zest of 6 oranges
1 cup granulated sugar
1 cup (2 sticks) plus 3 tablespoons, for coating pans, unsalted
*   butter, softened*
pinch of salt
1 cup chopped pecans

1. Prepare the cake pans following the same procedure as for Cinnamon Buns (see above).

2. Combine the orange zest and sugar in a food processor and process until the zest is finely ground, about 1 minute. Add the butter and salt. Process until smooth, and reserve.

About Rising

You need a draft-free area at about 80° to 90°F for proper rising. If your kitchen is too cold, you can place the dough inside the oven to rise. Just heat the oven to 150°F for about a minute. Renée also recommends sprinkling a gallon-size, strong plastic bag with flour. Place the dough inside, press out excess air and twist the bag closed near the top, leaving enough space for the dough to expand.

3. Follow steps 3 and 4 for Cinnamon Buns, for rolling and filling the dough, spreading half the orange zest mixture on each sheet and sprinkling each with ½ cup of nuts. Roll and cut dough and then cover with plastic wrap and a towel and set aside to rise in a warm place for half an hour.

4. Preheat oven to 350°F.

5. Bake for 20 to 25 minutes. Invert onto serving platter and make orange glaze while the rolls are cooling.

ORANGE GLAZE

4 tablespoons (½ stick) unsalted butter, softened
1¼ cups confectioners' sugar
3 tablespoons orange juice

Beat the butter until creamy. Add the sugar and beat until combined. Slowly add the orange juice, beating constantly until smooth. Pour the glaze over the warm rolls and serve.

Yields 14 to 18 rolls

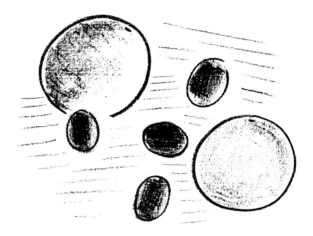

Tutti-frutti Muffins

Renée Carisio of Ma Cuisine

There's something cheerful and comforting about these muf
fins. We think what makes them so special is the sweet streusel topping and chunks of bright red berries in the cake.
They're ideal for afternoon snacks and early morning baking
in the summer, when berries are plentiful. Any combination
of fresh or frozen berries is fine. If you use frozen berries,
make sure to get them without syrup, whole, and freeze-dried
if possible.

1½ cups blueberries, strawberries and raspberries
2 tablespoons granulated sugar

Wash and dry the berries. If using strawberries, hull and slice
them. To sweeten the berries, mix them with sugar and let
stand 30 minutes for fresh, 5 minutes for frozen.

STREUSEL

½ cup granulated sugar
¼ cup all-purpose flour
4 tablespoons (½ stick) unsalted butter
1 teaspoon cinnamon
pinch of salt

Combine all the ingredients in a food processor. Process about
30 seconds, until crumbly, and set aside.

⅔ cup buttermilk
½ cup packed dark brown sugar
8 tablespoons (1 stick) unsalted butter
2 eggs
1 teaspoon vanilla extract
1¾ cups all-purpose flour
1½ teaspoons baking powder
1 teaspoon baking soda
¼ teaspoon salt

1. Preheat oven to 375°F. Grease or line muffin tins with
paper baking cups.

Food Processor Mixing

Most recipes for quickbreads and
muffins, and many for cookies and
cakes, can be adapted for the food
processor. As Renée explains it,
the key to mixing batter in the
food processor is remembering
that the machine turns five times
faster than an electric mixer, so it's
very easy to overprocess and get a
tough muffin. Always combine
liquid ingredients first and process
just until smooth. Then add the
dry ingredients and pulse only
until they disappear, about three
or four times. A pulse is no longer
than a second.

2. Combine the buttermilk, sugar, butter, eggs and vanilla in a food processor. Process about 30 seconds to combine. Add the flour, baking powder, baking soda and salt. Pulse 3 times, scrape down the sides and pulse once more.

3. Drain the berries. Stir them into the batter and spoon the batter into muffin cups until two-thirds full. Sprinkle about a tablespoon of streusel on top of each.

4. Bake for 25 minutes, or until a cake tester inserted in the center comes out clean.

Yields 14 muffins

SALADS

Garden Salad with Asparagus Sauce

Cecilia De Castro of Ma Cuisine

This colorful assortment of fresh vegetables in delicate asparagus sauce is a healthy, low-calorie food that doesn't forfeit taste or elegance. Use any assortment of seasonal vegetables in the salad, although you do need asparagus stalks for the sauce. Don't hesitate to trim down full-size vegetables if miniatures are hard to find. You can serve this versatile salad warm or chilled, as main course, appetizer or hors d'oeuvres.

GARDEN SALAD

1 pound asparagus
½ pound baby zucchini
4 ounces Chinese snow peas, tips trimmed and strings removed
1 bunch baby carrots, peeled and stems trimmed with ¼ inch of
* green remaining*
1 bunch baby turnips, stems trimmed
1 bunch baby beets, stems trimmed
1 basket cherry tomatoes

Wash and trim the vegetables. Cut off asparagus tips and reserve stalks for sauce. Blanch tips and all other vegetables (except the tomatoes), one vegetable at a time, in a pot of rapidly boiling salted water following these times: asparagus, zucchini and snow peas, 1 minute; carrots, 2 minutes; turnips and beets, 4 minutes. Rinse in cold water, pat dry and reserve.

ASPARAGUS SAUCE

3 tablespoons unsalted butter
2 shallots, minced
reserved asparagus stalks
½ cup dry white wine
2 cups chicken stock (page 224) or canned broth
2 tablespoons heavy cream
1 teaspoon fresh dill, minced, or ½ teaspoon dried
fresh lemon juice to taste
salt and freshly ground pepper to taste

1. Melt 1 tablespoon of the butter in a large skillet over medium-high heat. Sauté the shallots about 2 minutes. Add the asparagus stalks and cook about 2 minutes.

2. Pour in the wine, scraping the bottom of the pan to release the brown bits. Turn the heat to high and cook until the wine nearly evaporates. Add the chicken stock and bring to a boil. Reduce to a simmer and cook uncovered until the asparagus is tender, about half an hour.

3. Transfer the warm mixture to a food processor or blender. Add remaining butter and cream; puree until smooth. Strain through a fine sieve.

4. Return the mixture to the skillet. Add dill, season with lemon juice, salt and pepper to taste. Warm over low heat.

5. To serve: Arrange the vegetables on a large serving platter or on individual plates. Top with the warm sauce or serve the sauce in a bowl for dipping. Serve immediately or at room temperature.

Serves 4

How to Deglaze a Pan

Deglazing is the method used to release the hardened brown bits that stick to the bottom of the pan after sautéing. By releasing them you add their concentrated flavors to the sauce or stock that is being cooked.

First pour in the liquid to be reduced, then turn the heat to high and scrape the bottom of the pan with a wooden spoon or spatula to release the bits.

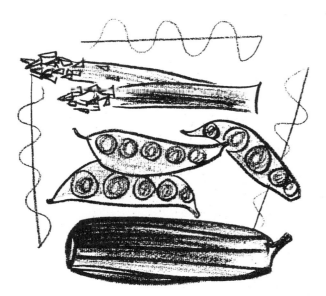

California Vegetable Salad with Avocado Vinaigrette

Jean-Pierre Lemanissier of Ma Maison

This was a favorite with Orson Welles who ate two meals a day at Ma Maison whenever he was in Los Angeles. Welles liked to order a double portion for lunch.

The dressing can be made a day in advance and refrigerated, and the vegetables can be blanched in advance and served at room temperature. Jean-Pierre recommends improvising with whatever vegetables are in season. You can serve this versatile dish as an appetizer at a dinner party, a main course salad at lunch, or a platter with the dressing in a separate dish at a cocktail party.

AVOCADO VINAIGRETTE

1 ripe avocado, peeled
2 tablespoons Dijon mustard
juice of 1 lemon
2 tablespoons sherry vinegar
6 tablespoons almond or corn oil
salt and white pepper to taste

1. Puree the avocado in a food processor or blender. Add the remaining ingredients and blend well.
2. Refrigerate a minimum of 1 hour.

VEGETABLE SALAD

1 cup cauliflowerettes
½ pound asparagus, trimmed and cut into 2-inch lengths
1 cup broccoli flowerettes
2 carrots, peeled and cut into 2-inch by ¼-inch sticks
4 ounces Chinese snow peas, ends trimmed and strings removed
1 yellow zucchini, sliced diagonally
1 green zucchini, sliced diagonally
1 head butterhead lettuce, washed and dried
1 head radicchio, washed and dried
1 head Belgian endive, washed and dried (garnish)

Perfect Blanched Vegetables

Blanched vegetables should be crisp, but not tough. Bring the water to a boil in a large saucepan, with a pinch or two of salt so the vegetables keep their bright colors. Then add the vegetables, one at a time, following the suggested cooking times. You can place them in a strainer for easy removal or use a slotted spoon to transfer them to a colander in the sink. Immediately rinse with cold water to stop the cooking. Pat the vegetables dry with paper towels.

1. Bring a large saucepan of salted water to a boil and blanch the vegetables following these cooking times; cauliflower, 5 minutes; asparagus, 4 minutes; broccoli and carrots, 3 minutes; snow peas, 2 minutes; zucchini, 1 minute. Immediately after blanching, refresh each vegetable under cold running water.

2. Break the lettuce and *radicchio* into bite-sized pieces and toss them in a small bowl. Divide the mixture and arrange on four salad plates. In another bowl, combine the blanched vegetables and enough avocado dressing to coat. Store any leftover dressing in a sealed container in the refrigerator for use on other salads. Divide the vegetables and arrange over the greens. Garnish with endive spears.

Serves 4

Ma Maison Chicken Salad

Jean-Pierre Lemanissier of Ma Maison

Perfect Poached Chicken
We like to poach chicken in stock
rather than water. The stock
infuses the meat with more flavor
and the resulting stock is double
strength.
In a stockpot or large saucepan
add just enough stock to cover the
chicken. Bring the liquid to a
simmer, *never* a boil, and cook at
a bare simmer for about twenty
minutes, uncovered. It is
important not to boil because
boiling contracts the fibers and
toughens the meat. Remove the
chicken from the pot to cool, to
stop the cooking immediately.

Ma Maison's chicken salad, like Nathan's hot dogs or Chasen's chili, is an institution. On the menu since the restaurant opened in 1973, this tangy version of an American classic has remained the most popular dish at lunch.

With a loaf of French bread, a light white wine and a fruit dessert, it would be a perfect hot weather lunch or supper. Store leftovers in the refrigerator for great chicken salad sandwiches.

1 (3 to 3½-pound) chicken
10 cups chicken stock (page 224) or canned chicken broth
1 Red or Golden Delicious apple, peeled, cored and diced
2 celery stalks, peeled and cubed
1 tablespoon capers, drained
½ cup mayonnaise (page 227)
2 tablespoons grainy mustard
2 tablespoons Dijon mustard
salt and freshly ground pepper to taste
fresh lemon juice to taste
1 head butter or limestone lettuce, washed and dried
¼ cup vinaigrette (page 228)
2 hard-boiled eggs, halved (garnish)
2 tomatoes, cut in wedges (garnish)
2 bell peppers, sliced (garnish)
8 ounces green beans, blanched (garnish)

1. Combine the chicken and stock in a large pot. Bring to a simmer and cook uncovered for 20 minutes over low heat.

2. Remove the chicken from the pot to cool. When it's cool enough to handle, but still warm, remove and discard the skin. Pull the meat from the bones and shred by hand into bite-sized pieces. Place the pieces in a large mixing bowl.

3. Add the apple, celery, capers, mayonnaise and mustards to the chicken and combine gently. Taste and adjust seasonings with salt, pepper and lemon juice.

4. Break the lettuce into bite-sized pieces and place in another mixing bowl. Toss with the vinaigrette.

5. To serve: Divide the lettuce among four serving plates. Top each with a serving of chicken salad and garnish as desired. Serve at room temperature.

Serves 4

Grilled Chicken and Goat Cheese Salad*

Michael McCarty of Michael's

How to Fan an Avocado
Place an avocado half, cut side
down, on a serving plate or
counter. Cut into thin lengthwise
slices, leaving about half an inch
intact at the narrow end. With
your fingers, spread the slices into
a fan shape.

This is the kind of dish that Michael serves when he invites friends for Sunday brunch. Although the ingredient list is long, the technique is uncomplicated and most things can be chopped and combined in advance and assembled while the chicken is grilling.

The beauty of this salad lies in the variety of little tastes carefully arranged on the plate, so try to use extra large dinner plates or platters. Any white wine goes well with this casual lunch dish.

JALAPEÑO CILANTRO SALSA

¼ cup olive oil
juice of 2 limes
1 bunch cilantro, or Chinese parsley, stems removed and coarsely
    chopped
1 jalapeño pepper, roasted, peeled, seeded (page 14) and finely
    chopped
salt and freshly ground pepper to taste

Combine the ingredients in a small bowl and set aside.

TOMATO CONCASSÉ

3 medium tomatoes, peeled, seeded and diced (page 19)
2 tablespoons fresh basil, stems removed and chopped
salt and freshly ground pepper to taste

Toss the ingredients in a small bowl and set aside.

BALSAMIC VINAIGRETTE

½ cup olive oil
3 tablespoons balsamic vinegar
salt and freshly ground pepper to taste

Whisk the ingredients together and set aside.

*From *Michael's Cookbook* by Michael McCarty.

GREEN SALAD

1 head limestone lettuce
2 bunches mâche *or lamb's lettuce (page 228)*
1 bunch arugula
1 head red leaf lettuce
1 head radicchio

Separate all the leafy greens, wash and dry. Tear the leaves into bite-sized pieces, toss with the vinaigrette and reserve.

6 boneless chicken breast halves, skins on
1 (12-ounce) log soft goat cheese, such as Montrachet, cut in 1/2-
 inch round slices
olive oil for brushing
salt and freshly ground pepper to taste
3 red bell peppers, cored, seeded and coarsely julienned
3 yellow bell peppers, cored, seeded and coarsely julienned
1 large sweet onion, in 1/2-*inch slices*
3 avocados

1. Preheat grill or broiler.
2. With your fingers, gently make a pocket between the skin and meat of each breast, inserting your finger along the long side of each breast and leaving the skin attached along the other edges. Place a goat cheese slice inside the pocket. Brush lightly with olive oil; sprinkle with salt and pepper.
3. Brush the pepper strips and onion slices with olive oil and season with salt and pepper. Set aside.
4. Grill or broil the breasts until well browned, about 7 minutes per side; begin with skin side down if grilling.
5. While the chicken is cooking, cut the avocados in half, peel and pit them and then cut into fan (page 76).
6. About 1 minute before the chicken is done, grill the pepper and onion slices for about 1 minute or broil for 3 minutes. The vegetables should be heated through and lightly charred.
7. To serve: Divide the tossed green salad and arrange in the center of each large serving plate. Cut each grilled breast into four or five slices, across the width, and place each portion on top of the bed of greens. Garnish each plate with a fanned avocado half; three small mounds of tomato *concassé*, and the grilled peppers and onions. Spoon the *salsa* over the chicken and serve while the chicken is warm.

Serves 6

Warm Chicken Salad with Gorgonzola Dressing

Antonio Orlando of Primi

Blue-Veined Cheeses

Although all blue cheeses are strong tasting, there are subtle differences among the types available. Italian Gorgonzola is available in a creamy, sweet variety called *dolce latte* and a stronger, saltier type called *picante*. *Picante* has a crumbly, dry consistency. English Stilton is harder than Gorgonzola, and is made from richer milk. It has a slight cheddar flavor. French Roquefort is made from unskimmed sheep's milk. Different brands have their distinctive characteristics, but as a rule Roquefort is saltier and more pungent than the others. Blue cheese can be an elegant ending to a special dinner. Serve it with a selection of fruits and nuts, some thinly sliced crusty bread and a glass of port or mellow red wine.

This light chicken salad is special enough to be served as a main course, but you can also present it at the beginning of an elegant dinner party. Antonio recommends using imported Gorgonzola *dolce latte.* It's creamier and sweeter than the domestic kind.

3 whole chicken breasts
1 onion, quartered
1 carrot, peeled and cut in 1-inch lengths
1 celery stalk, cut in 1-inch lengths
1 sprig fresh thyme
1 bay leaf

1. Poach the chicken breasts by covering them with water in a large saucepan (page 74). Add the onion, carrot, celery, thyme and bay leaf. Bring the water almost to a boil; reduce to a simmer and cook for 20 minutes, uncovered.

2. Remove the breasts and set aside to cool. Then remove the skin, take the meat off the bone and julienne the chicken in ¼-inch strips; reserve.

SALAD

1 head radicchio *or red oak leaf lettuce (page 228)*
1 head curly endive or chicory
2 bunches arugula, *stems removed*
2 tomatoes, peeled, seeded and julienned (See page 101 for how to julienne tomatoes)

Wash and dry the salad greens. Slice into ¾-inch strips and toss in a large salad bowl with the tomatoes.

GORGONZOLA DRESSING

½ cup virgin olive oil
½ cup white wine vinegar
1 teaspoon fresh chopped thyme
1 teaspoon fresh chopped tarragon
½ pound Gorgonzola dolce latte, *crumbled*
salt and freshly ground pepper to taste

1. To make the dressing: Combine the oil, vinegar and herbs in a medium saucepan. Cook over medium-high heat for about 1 minute. Remove from heat and whisk in the cheese until smooth. Season to taste with salt and pepper.

2. To assemble the salad: Toss and coat the salad greens with about a quarter of the warm dressing. Arrange the strips of chicken on top and drizzle with the remaining dressing. Serve immediately.

Serves 6 as a main course

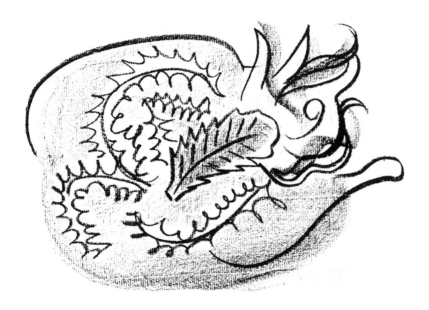

Warm Salad of Stuffed Chicken Breasts with Raspberry-Walnut Dressing

Roy Yamaguchi of 385 North

Before he started his own restaurant when he was twenty-seven, Roy Yamaguchi trained at the Culinary Institute of America in New York. He also cooked at a number of Los Angeles restaurants, including L'Ermitage, where he perfected his technique working alongside Michel Blanchet.

This is a challenging dish to prepare, but things can be simplified if you cook the stuffed chicken rolls in advance, seal and refrigerate them and gently warm in water just before serving. The stuffing is called a *mousseline* in French cuisine.

STUFFED CHICKEN BREASTS

6 whole chicken breasts, boneless and skinless
1 cup heavy cream, cold
1 egg, cold
½ cup shelled, unsalted pistachio nuts
1 bunch fresh basil, stems removed and thinly sliced
1 ear of corn, kernels only, or ½ cup canned corn
2 artichoke bottoms, (fresh, thawed frozen or canned), diced
¾ teaspoon salt
¾ teaspoon pepper
1 quart chicken stock (page 224) or canned chicken broth

1. To make the stuffing: Chill processor bowl for about an hour before using. Then puree 3 whole chicken breasts until smooth, about 2 minutes. Add the cream and egg; process until combined, about 30 seconds. The mixture should look like stiffly beaten cream.

2. In a large mixing bowl, combine the pureed chicken mixture with the nuts, basil, corn, artichokes, salt and pepper. Reserve in the refrigerator.

3. To make the rolls: Slice the remaining 3 chicken breasts in half to make 6 half-breasts. Flatten to ⅛-inch thickness, by placing the chicken between two sheets of plastic wrap and pounding with the flat side of a mallet. Place six 10-inch rectangles of plastic wrap on a flat surface, and place a chicken breast on top of each. Spoon an equal amount of the stuffing

mixture on each breast. Roll the breast around the stuffing to form a tight cylinder; wrap in plastic wrap and seal by twisting the plastic ends.

4. In a large pot, bring the stock to a simmer; drop in chicken rolls and poach for about 10 minutes. Remove the plastic by lifting each roll out with a slotted spoon and tugging at the ends. Return rolls to the stock and continue to simmer for 10 minutes more. Remove the rolls with a slotted spoon. They should feel spongy when pressed between two fingers. Set aside or wrap and refrigerate if preparing in advance.

SALAD

1 head escarole
1 head radicchio *(page 228)*
1 head red leaf lettuce or mâche

Wash and dry the salad greens. Tear in bite-sized pieces. Mix in a large salad bowl and reserve.

DRESSING

⅓ cup walnut oil
1 teaspoon minced garlic
8 ounces mushrooms, thinly sliced
¼ cup raspberry vinegar

1. To make the dressing: Heat the oil in a medium-sized skillet over high heat until it starts to smoke. Lower the heat; add the garlic and mushrooms; sauté until soft. Remove from heat and stir in the vinegar.

2. Toss the salad with the dressing. Slice the chicken rolls in ½-inch slices, arrange on top of the salad and serve.

Serves 6

Preparing a Mousseline

The French term *mousseline* refers to a mixture of raw chicken or fish pureed with cream and egg. *Mousselines* are typically used to make terrines and stuffings.

The food processor makes it possible to make a delicate *mousseline* in seconds. However, since the motor turns at about 1700 rpm and creates heat as it turns, there is always a danger of actually "cooking" the delicate ingredients. To avoid this, always make sure that all the ingredients as well as the processor bowl are *well chilled*. Process for no longer than the time called for in the recipe.

Smoked Chicken Salad with Julienned Vegetables

Celestino Drago of Celestino's

This is no ordinary chicken salad, but one with a smoky taste of chicken, crunchy vegetables and creamy dressing.

The salad may be tossed with the dressing and refrigerated until serving time. Celestino suggests taking this along on your next picnic with a loaf of Italian bread and a bottle of cold Chardonnay.

1 (4-pound) smoked chicken, skin and bones removed
2 carrots, peeled
4 ounces snow peas, strings removed
1 zucchini
1 head romaine lettuce
½ cup pine nuts, toasted (page 206)
6 sun-dried tomatoes

1. Slice the chicken against the grain in ¼-inch slices. Stack the slices and julienne.

2. Chop the carrots in 2-inch lengths and julienne. Slice the snow peas in half lengthwise. With the skins on, slice the outer quarter inch of the zucchini and remove and discard the core. Julienne remaining zucchini.

3. In a large pot of rapidly boiling salted water blanch the carrots for 2 minutes, snow peas and zucchini for 1 minute. Rinse with cold water and reserve.

4. Wash and dry the lettuce and slice in ¼-inch strips. Julienne the tomatoes.

Sun-Dried Tomatoes

Sun-dried tomatoes add a very concentrated, salty flavor to the chicken salad. They are usually imported from Italy, where they're slowly baked in the sun and then packed in olive oil. Antonio Orlando of Valentino's tells us that in Italy home cooks have been making their own sun-dried tomatoes for years. They simply sprinkle salt on split tomato halves and set them out in the sun to dry for about two weeks. He suggests combining them with dried black olives, anchovies, ricotta cheese and basil for an easy pasta sauce. Experiment with the intense flavor of these tomatoes on pizzas and in other salads and pasta sauces.

MAYONNAISE DILL DRESSING

1 egg yolk
2 tablespoons mayonnaise
2 tablespoons sour cream
1½ teaspoons Dijon mustard
1½ cups olive oil
2 tablespoons fresh dill, chopped
salt and freshly ground pepper to taste

1. In a food processor or with a whisk, combine egg yolk, mayonnaise, sour cream and mustard. With the machine running, or whisking constantly, add the oil in a slow steady stream. Stir in the dill and season to taste with salt and pepper.

2. To assemble the salad: Divide the romaine and arrange on six plates. In a large mixing bowl combine chicken, all the vegetables, pine nuts, sun-dried tomatoes and dressing. Toss to coat the salad and arrange on top of each bed of lettuce.

Serves 6

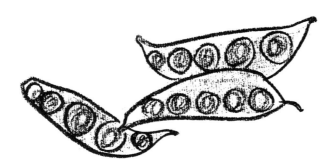

Asian Grilled Duck Salad

Roy Yamaguchi of 385 North

Cooking with Duck
Although duck is gaining in
popularity, it's still not available
cut in parts in the supermarket.
Ask your butcher to bone the
breasts and remove the legs, and
to save the carcass for you as well.
Legs can be used in this recipe,
the breasts in another, more
elegant recipe (page 109), and the
carcass may be used for making
stock.
Cracklings, or fried duck skins,
can add flavor and crunch to your
favorite salad. Simply slice the
excess skin into thin strips. Sauté
the strips in a hot, dry skillet until
crisp and toss in your salad.

The Japanese word for barbecue is *yakitori*, literally "grilled birds." In this tribute to his native Japan, Roy Yamaguchi weaves the sweet taste of honey and papaya with light salad greens and hearty duck.

As with many recipes from 385 North this can be served as an appetizer or a main course. Substitute cantaloupe or mango if papaya is unavailable.

4 duck legs

MARINADE

1 cup soy sauce
1 tablespoon sesame oil (page 93)
½ cup granulated sugar
2 teaspoons fresh ginger, minced
1 teaspoon garlic, minced
grated zest of 1 orange

Combine the marinade ingredients in a small bowl. Add duck, cover and marinate for ½ hour at room temperature. Prepare the salad and dressing while the duck is marinating.

SALAD

5 ounces Chinese long beans or green beans
1 small head red leaf lettuce
1 small head radicchio (page 228)
1 small head Boston lettuce
1 papaya, peeled, seeded, chopped in ½-inch chunks

Slice the beans diagonally in 2-inch pieces. Blanch in rapidly boiling water for 2 minutes. Refresh immediately in cold water. Wash and dry the salad greens. Tear into bite-sized pieces and mix in salad bowl with papaya and beans.

DRESSING

2 tablespoons sherry wine vinegar
2 tablespoons honey
2 tablespoons sesame oil
2 tablespoons walnut oil

1. Whisk the vinegar and honey in a small bowl until combined. Whisk in the oils and reserve.
2. Grill or broil duck legs for 10 minutes on each side. Toss the salad with dressing while the duck is cooking. Remove the duck meat from the bone by slicing it against the grain. Stack and julienne in thin strips. Scatter on top of salad.

Serves 4 to 6

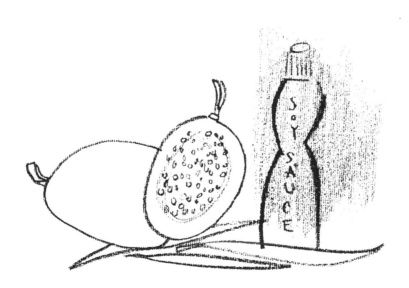

Salad with Poached Eggs and Hot Bacon Bits

Jean-François Meteigner of L'Orangerie

Don't let the idea of poached eggs on a green salad turn you away from this recipe. It's delicious. Jean-François suggests serving this classic French appetizer at the start of a light fish dinner. It's important to use a lettuce as stiff as curly endive; a softer lettuce will wilt under the heat of the bacon.

½ pound thick sliced bacon, cut in ½-inch squares
2 bunches curly endive (page 228)
½ cup red wine vinegar
6 tablespoons bacon drippings
salt and freshly ground pepper to taste
8 large eggs
1 cup white wine vinegar
3 cups water
1 bunch fresh chives, finely minced (garnish)

1. Fry the bacon until crisp. Drain on paper towels and reserve the drippings.

2. Tear the endive into bite-sized pieces, discarding the green outer leaves, using white part only. Wash and dry.

3. Toss the endive in a large bowl with the red wine vinegar, bacon and bacon drippings. Season with salt and pepper to taste.

4. Divide the salad among four plates.

5. Bring the white wine vinegar and water to a simmer in a skillet. Poach the eggs in this mixture for 1 to 2 minutes. When the eggs are ready, remove with a slotted spoon and place two on top of each salad. Garnish with minced chives and serve immediately.

Serves 4

How to Poach an Egg

You don't need any special equipment to make perfect poached eggs. A medium-sized skillet with straight sides will do. Just simmer the water and vinegar mixture over low heat. The vinegar is used to set the egg whites. Gently add the eggs one at a time and cook each for 2 minutes, maximum. The whites should just set and the yolks remain runny.

Grapefruit Salad with Fresh Mint
Michel Blanchet of L'Ermitage

Michel Blanchet combines grapefruit and mint for the lightest, coolest salad imaginable. He serves it very cold at the restaurant and suggests you chill it for three to four hours so the flavor of mint saturates the grapefruit. This low-calorie fruit dish makes an elegant appetizer or a refresher between courses.

2 pink grapefruits
2 white grapefruits
10 mint leaves, finely chopped
4 strawberries, hulled

1. Peel the grapefruits over a bowl, reserving the juice. Section the fruits by slicing between the membranes with a sharp paring knife. Reserve the fruit and juice separately.

2. Mix the mint with the grapefruit juice and set aside.

3. Arrange alternate pink and white grapefruit slices in a circular pattern on four serving plates. Place a strawberry in the center, spoon the reserved juice over the sections and refrigerate for 3 to 4 hours.

Serves 4

How to Supreme a Fruit

This method of removing perfect sections of citrus fruits is known as supreming. Work with a small, sharp knife or a serrated blade over a bowl to catch the juices. Start by slicing off the top and bottom with flat horizontal slices. Then run your knife in a circular pattern between the pith and the fruit, removing both the peel and the white part. When only the fruit remains, make a slice on either side of each membrane to loosen the section. Reserve the sections in one bowl and the juice in another so you can easily strain the juice of seeds.

Wild Mountain Salad with Honey-Mustard Dressing

Ed La Dou of Caioti

Ed combines a variety of distinctive lettuces in this simple green salad. Other sharp-tasting greens may be substituted for those in this recipe—turnip greens, mustard greens, spinach or kale would be good. Always use the freshest greens and be careful not to cover their flavors with too much dressing. The honey-mustard dressing, which can be kept in the refrigerator for a couple of weeks, provides a sweet counterpoint to the peppery greens.

1 bunch dandelion greens or curly endive
1 head red chard, ribs removed
1 head radicchio *(page 228)*
2 bunches watercress
2 bunches mâche *or lamb's lettuce*
2 bunches arugula
10–12 nasturtium blossoms (garnish)

Remove all of the stems and cores of the leafy greens. Tear into bite-sized pieces, rinse and soak in cold water for 15 minutes to remove all soil. Dry in salad spinner or pat dry with paper towels. Transfer to salad bowl.

HONEY-MUSTARD DRESSING

2 shallots, minced
2 garlic cloves, minced
3 tablespoons honey
2 tablespoons grainy mustard
½ cup sherry vinegar
juice of 1 lemon
1 cup extra virgin olive oil

1. Combine all the ingredients except the oil in a mixing bowl. Whisk together. Slowly drizzle in the oil, whisking constantly to combine.

2. Toss the salad with enough dressing to coat the leaves. Remove the petals from the nasturtium blossoms and sprinkle them on top of the salad as a garnish. Any leftover dressing may be stored in a sealed container in the refrigerator for a couple of weeks.

Serves 8

Warm Lobster and Orange Salad

Jean-François Meteigner of L'Orangerie

The inspiration for this elegant warm salad is the French region of Brittany, famous for its abundance of shellfish and the creativity of its chefs.

You can substitute other greens if *mâche* is not available, but it's important to serve this salad quickly, or the croutons and lettuce will get soggy from the heat of the dressing. Also, be careful not to overcook the lobster since it will be "cooked" again in the dressing. Follow this elegant appetizer with a fish entrée or serve as a main course for lunch with some crusty French bread.

1 small orange
1 (1½-pound) lobster or 1 (8-ounce) frozen lobster tail
1 slice white bread, crusts removed
1 tablespoon unsalted butter
½ cup extra virgin olive oil
1 shallot, minced
2 teaspoons fresh dill, chopped
1 head mâche *or lamb's lettuce, washed and dried*
salt and freshly ground pepper to taste

1. Remove the orange zest with a vegetable peeler, being careful not to remove the white pith. Squeeze the juice and reserve for dressing. Stack the strips of zest and julienne in ⅙- × 2-inch strips. Blanch for 2 minutes in boiling water. Reserve.

2. Bring a large stockpot of water to a boil. Cook the lobster for only 3 minutes. Rinse in cold water until the lobster is cool enough to handle.

3. Remove the tail and claws, crack the shell and extract the meat. Cut in ½-inch slices and reserve. The body and head may be frozen and used for making sauce or bisque.

4. Cut the bread in ½-inch cubes. Melt the butter in a 10-inch sauté pan over medium heat and sauté the bread cubes until golden, 2 to 3 minutes. Remove from pan and reserve.

5. In a mixing bowl, whisk together the orange juice, olive oil, shallot and dill. Pour dressing into the sauté pan with the reserved lobster and orange zest. Warm over low heat for 2 minutes.

6. Break the lettuce into bite-sized pieces and divide between two serving plates. Top with the warm lobster and dressing to taste. Scatter the croutons around the outside edges and serve immediately.

Serves 2

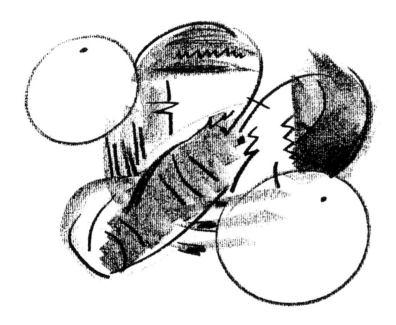

Panzanella

Evan Kleiman of Angeli

How to Seed a Cucumber
Peel the cucumber with a
vegetable peeler or a small paring
knife. Cut in half lengthwise.
Scoop out the seeds by running a
melon baller or teaspoon along
the inside core.

Panzanella has been on the menu since Angeli opened in December 1984 and remains one of the most popular salads at the restaurant. It's Tuscan home cooking at its best—simple, inexpensive and delicious.

Serve this substantial salad at lunch with a light *frittata* (an Italian-style omelet) or at dinnertime with any roasted or grilled meat. You can make the tomato mixture up to a day in advance, but don't assemble until right before serving, so the bread doesn't get too limp.

6 slices, ½-inch thick, day-old French or Italian country bread
6 tomatoes, peeled, seeded, and cut in ½-inch dice
2 tablespoons capers, drained
½ cup extra virgin olive oil
¼ cup red wine vinegar
salt and freshly ground pepper to taste
2 cucumbers, peeled, halved and seeded, and cut in ½-inch dice
¼ red onion, thinly sliced (optional)
2 red or green bell peppers, cored, seeded and finely julienned

1. Cut the bread into 1-inch strips. Reserve.

2. In a glass or stainless steel bowl mix together the tomatoes, capers, oil, vinegar, salt and pepper. The tomato mixture may be made up to a day ahead. If refrigerated, bring back to room temperature before using.

3. To assemble the salad: Place the bread strips on a large platter. Scatter the cucumbers, onion if desired, and bell pepper over the bread. Pour the tomato mixture with all the accumulated juices over the bread and vegetables. Serve at room temperature.

Serves 8 to 10

Oriental Pork Salad

Renée Carisio of Ma Cuisine

Crisp, blanched vegetables and tender strips of roast pork are tossed with an easy Chinese-style dressing in this substantial main-course salad. Don't overcook the pork. Tenderloin, the choicest cut, is exceptionally tender and juicy. Extra pork slices are excellent on egg bun sandwiches with barbecue sauce.

1 pound pork tenderloin

MARINADE

2 garlic cloves, crushed
1 teaspoon fresh ginger, minced
1 scallion, green and white parts, minced
¼ cup dry sherry or Chinese rice wine
¼ cup soy sauce
3 tablespoons hoisin sauce (available at Oriental markets)

1. Combine the marinade ingredients in a small bowl. Place the pork in a ceramic or glass baking dish. Pour the marinade over the pork and marinate a minimum of 4 hours, refrigerated.

2. After the pork has marinated, preheat oven to 450°F.

3. Place the pork on a rack in a roasting pan, reserving the marinade for use in the dressing. Roast for 30 minutes. Set aside to cool. Cut in ¼-inch slices; stack the slices and julienne. Reserve.

SALAD

1 pound asparagus, trimmed and chopped in 2-inch lengths
½ pound Chinese snow peas, trimmed and chopped in half, lengthwise
1 red bell pepper, cored, seeded and julienned
1 yellow bell pepper, cored, seeded and julienned
3 scallions, green and white parts, chopped in 2-inch lengths and slivered

Chinese Sesame Oil

Due to its low burning point sesame oil is never used for stir-frying. It is always added after the food has been cooked. The sesame oil called for in Oriental recipes is made from roasted seeds and is dark brown. American sesame oil is golden and is made from raw seeds.

When purchasing Chinese sesame oil open the cap and smell the oil. If it smells burnt, it means the oil was made from burnt sesame seeds and won't have the desired flavor. Keep looking and smelling!

1. Steam the asparagus and snow peas for approximately 2 minutes. Refresh with cold water.

2. Mix all the vegetables with the pork strips in a large salad or mixing bowl.

ORIENTAL DRESSING

3 tablespoons marinade
3 tablespoons hoisin sauce
1 tablespoon fresh lemon juice
1 tablespoon sesame oil
1 teaspoon chili paste with garlic (optional) (available at Oriental markets)
½ cup vegetable or safflower oil

1. Combine the marinade, hoisin, lemon juice, sesame oil and chili paste in a food processor or blender. Add the vegetable oil in a slow, steady stream with the machine running.

2. Toss the salad with the dressing and serve at room temperature or chilled.

Serves 6

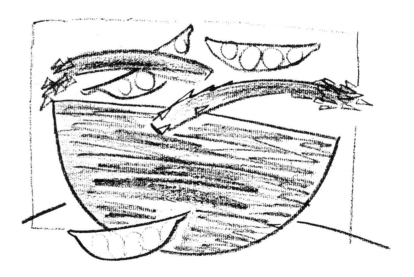

Warm Scallop Salad with Saffron Sauce

Celestino Drago of Celestino's

This delicate, warm salad seems inspired more by Celestino's time in California than by his native Italy. Italian salads are traditionally simple combinations of leafy vegetables tossed with olive oil and vinegar. This exceptionally sophisticated salad would make a good beginning to a formal dinner party.

SALAD

2 tablespoons unsalted butter
4 heads Belgian endive, cut in ¼-inch horizontal slices
2 bunches arugula, *stems removed (page 228)*
2 small red bell peppers, cored, seeded and cut in ¼-inch dice
1 tablespoon fresh lemon juice
4 teaspoons beluga caviar (optional)
1 pound sea scallops, muscles removed

1. Melt 1 tablespoon of the butter in a large skillet over medium heat. Sauté the endive, *arugula* and red peppers until wilted, about 2 minutes. Sprinkle with lemon juice and caviar and reserve in a bowl.
2. Slice the scallops in half horizontally.
3. Melt the remaining tablespoon of butter in the same skillet and sauté the scallops over medium heat until lightly browned on both sides, about 3 minutes. Reserve.

SAFFRON SAUCE

1 teaspoon saffron threads
1 tablespoon unsalted butter
1 small shallot, minced
¼ cup brandy
½ cup dry white wine
2 cups heavy cream
salt and white pepper to taste

1. Dissolve the saffron threads in ½ tablespoon warm water for 5 minutes.
2. Melt the butter in a medium-sized skillet over medium heat. Sauté the shallot until golden, about 1 minute. Add

Cooking with Wine

Always use a palatable wine when cooking. Don't use a wine that isn't good enough to drink, because when you boil away the alcohol, all that remains is the concentrated flavor of the wine. Avoid "cooking" wines since they're usually of inferior quality and have salt added.

brandy and wine; turn heat to high and cook until the liquid in the pan is reduced to a thick and syrupy consistency.

3. Add the saffron and cream. Cook until the liquid in the pan is reduced by half. Sauce should be pale yellow. Season with salt and pepper to taste.

4. To serve: Divide the warm salad mixture among four serving plates. Place the scallops on top, drizzle with the sauce and serve immediately.

Serves 4

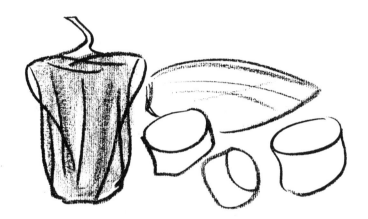

Scallop Salad with Spinach and Roasted Peppers

Michael Feig of Country Fresh Herbs

Michael created this colorful salad to satisfy the demand at Ma Maison for healthy, light meals in the middle of the day. An easy dish to prepare, the peppers can be roasted, the vegetables chopped and the dressing mixed in advance. Sauté the scallops and assemble the salad just before serving to keep the spinach from wilting.

CAESAR DRESSING

2 anchovy fillets, mashed
2 garlic cloves, minced
¼ cup freshly grated Parmesan cheese
1 tablespoon Dijon mustard
¼ cup sherry wine vinegar
¾ cup extra virgin olive oil
salt and freshly ground pepper to taste

Combine anchovies, garlic, cheese and mustard in a mixing bowl. Whisk in the vinegar. Add the olive oil in a slow steady stream, whisking constantly. Season to taste with salt and pepper; reserve.

SALAD

3 bell peppers, preferably red, green and yellow
1 bunch spinach, washed, dried and sliced into 1-inch strips
1 carrot, peeled and cut in thin circles
1 tomato, peeled, seeded and julienned (page 101)
2 tablespoons olive oil
12 ounces bay scallops, muscles removed

1. Roast the peppers over a gas flame or under a well-heated broiler (page 14). Peel, seed and slice into julienne strips. Reserve.
2. Prepare the spinach, carrot and tomato, reserving each individually.

About Scallops

In most recipes, sea scallops and bay scallops can be used interchangeably. We prefer sea scallops for more luxurious dishes and bay scallops for casual meals. To prepare either, remove the small opaque muscle on the side by gently pulling.

When substituting the larger sea scallops for bay, you can follow the same cooking time called for in your recipe by cutting the scallops in quarter-inch horizontal slices, or you can leave them whole and increase the cooking time by three to four minutes. When substituting small bay for sea scallops, cooking time is always about two minutes. To test either for doneness, cut a scallop in half. If the center is opaque, the fish is done.

3. Heat the oil in a medium skillet over high heat. Sauté the scallops until just opaque, about 2 minutes.

4. To assemble: Toss the spinach with ¼ cup dressing. Divide and place at the center of four serving plates. Place the pepper strips over the spinach. Spoon the scallops over the peppers and garnish the rim of the plate with bits of carrot and tomato. Sprinkle with dressing to taste.

Serves 4

Warm Shrimp Salad with Basil Vinaigrette Dressing

Jean-François Meteigner of L'Orangerie

Jean-François takes great care in food's visual presentation at L'Orangerie. In fact, when he teaches this recipe at the school, it's accompanied by a diagram, so that students can duplicate the restaurant's presentation.

Chicory, Belgian endive or Bibb lettuce work well if some of the other lettuces are difficult to find. The chef suggests using only the heart of each lettuce. You'll need four bamboo skewers for the shrimp. Let the skewers soak in water for an hour before using if you plan to grill, to avoid a burnt flavor.

8 very large shrimp, peeled and deveined

MARINADE

½ cup olive oil
1 bunch fresh basil, chopped
½ teaspoon salt
¼ teaspoon pepper

Place 2 shrimps on each skewer. Combine the marinade ingredients in a glass or ceramic bowl; add the shrimp and let stand for 1 hour at room temperature.

SALAD

2 tablespoons unsalted butter
2 red bell peppers, cored, seeded and julienned
2 green bell peppers, cored, seeded and julienned
1 bunch arugula
2 ounces mâche or lamb's lettuce (page 228)
1 head red leaf lettuce

1. Melt the butter in a medium-sized skillet over low heat. Cook the red and green peppers until soft, about 10 minutes. Reserve.

2. Wash and dry the salad greens. Tear into bite-sized pieces. Combine in a mixing bowl and reserve.

How to Julienne a Pepper
Cut out and discard the top and bottom of the pepper. Then make one vertical cut along a rib to open, and discard the seeds and inner membrane. Flatten the pepper with one hand and slice in eighth-inch vertical strips.

BASIL VINAIGRETTE

½ cup red wine vinegar
2 shallots
1 garlic clove
2 bunches fresh basil, stems removed
1½ cups extra virgin olive oil
salt and freshly ground pepper to taste

1. To make the dressing: In a blender or food processor, combine the vinegar, shallots, garlic and basil until smooth. With the machine running, gradually add the oil in a slow steady stream. Add salt and pepper to taste and reserve.

2. Grill or broil the shrimp on the skewers for about 2 minutes on each side. If broiling, the tray should be about 4 inches away from the heat.

3. Toss the salad greens with just enough dressing to coat the leaves; divide among four serving plates. Line the sautéed peppers along one side of the plate. Top each plate with a skewer of shrimp, drizzle on some of the remaining dressing and serve immediately.

Serves 4

Salad of Chopped Veal, Olives and Tomatoes

Antonio Orlando of Primi

In this recipe Antonio has updated the classic Italian dish *vitello tonnato*. This salad tastes best cold. Any leftover dressing can be tossed with a short pasta like rigatoni for a delicious cold pasta dish.

1½ pounds veal roast, top round
1 carrot, peeled and cut in 1-inch lengths
1 celery stalk, cut in 1-inch lengths
1 onion, quartered
2 sprigs fresh rosemary
salt and freshly ground pepper to taste
¾ cup dry white wine

To roast the veal: Preheat oven to 350°F. Place the veal in a roasting pan with all the vegetables. Place the rosemary on top of the veal and sprinkle with salt and pepper. Pour in the wine and roast for 1 hour. The meat should be a little pink inside when done. Set aside to cool and then slice in ¼-inch slices and julienne into strips.

SALAD

2 heads Belgian endive or butterleaf lettuce
1 bunch spinach
1 head radicchio or red oak leaf lettuce (page 228)
½ cup green olives, sliced
2 tomatoes, peeled and julienned (see note)

Wash and dry the salad greens. Slice into ¾-inch strips and toss with the olives and tomatoes.

TUNA DRESSING

1 (7-ounce) can tuna, packed in oil
½ cup dry white wine
juice of ½ lemon
1 tablespoon capers, drained
2 cornichons
2 anchovy fillets
1 cup Homemade Mayonnaise (page 227)

How to Julienne a Tomato
Peel the tomato and cut it into quarters. Cut out and discard the interior of the tomato and wipe out any remaining seeds with your fingers. Only the exterior of the tomato should remain. Stack the pieces and slice into quarter-inch-thick strips.

1. To make the dressing: In a food processor or a blender, puree all the dressing ingredients except the mayonnaise until combined. Pour into a large mixing bowl and gradually whisk in the mayonnaise until combined.

2. To assemble the salad: Toss and coat the salad greens with about 1 cup of tuna dressing. Arrange the veal strips on top and add more dressing to taste. The leftover salad dressing can be kept in a sealed container in the refrigerator for about four days.

Serves 6

ENTREES

Roast Chicken with Garlic and Fresh Herbs

Renée Carisio of Ma Cuisine

Free-Range Chickens

Chickens labeled *free range* have been raised on smaller ranches where they are given more space to roam and are fed grain rather than the animal protein and hormones the average chicken feeds on. As a result the meat has a gamier, more natural flavor than the chicken we are accustomed to eating. They cost a bit more, but are still less expensive per pound than most beef, veal, lamb or seafood. Try your local health food market if these chickens are unavailable at your butcher shop or supermarket.

When Jacques Pepin visited the school, he showed Renée this simple technique for perfect roast chicken. As the butter melts underneath the skin, it continually bastes the chicken and brings the flavor of fresh herbs and garlic to every part. Renée favors the Italian combination of rosemary, thyme and sage with chicken, but feel free to experiment with your own favorite herbs—basil, parsley and tarragon are possibilities.

1 (3½-pound) chicken
6 tablespoons unsalted butter, room temperature
1½ tablespoons fresh thyme, finely chopped
1½ tablespoons fresh rosemary, finely chopped
1½ tablespoons fresh sage, finely chopped
2 garlic cloves, finely minced
½ teaspoon salt
¼ teaspoon freshly ground pepper

1. Preheat oven to 425°F.

2. Combine all the ingredients—except the chicken, of course—in a small bowl. Mash the mixture with a fork to form a paste.

3. Remove any excess fat from the chicken's tail and neck area. Loosen the skin by carefully running your fingers between the skin and meat along the breast, legs and thighs. Divide the butter and herb paste into four parts. Stuff one portion into each leg and breast. Press the skin with your fingers to distribute the paste evenly. Sprinkle the outside of the chicken with salt and pepper to taste.

4. Place in a roasting pan and roast for 20 minutes on each side and 20 minutes breast up, for a total of 1 hour. This technique will keep the chicken from drying out. Basting is not required, since the butter melting beneath the skin keeps the bird moist. Set aside to cool for 15 minutes before slicing.

Serves 4

Spicy City Chicken

Susan Feniger and Mary Sue Milliken of City Restaurant

Unlike some Indian cooking in America, which tends to be overwhelmingly hot, this grilled chicken dish is a subtle blend of sweet and spicy. Susan combines *jalapeños* and *cilantro* with sugar, eggs and vinegar for a sauce that is exciting without being overpowering.

At the restaurant it's served on a bed of Basmati rice (page 46). The chefs suggest serving it with beer or a strong-bodied Chardonnay.

3 pounds boneless chicken, breasts and thighs
salt and freshly ground pepper to taste
6 scallions, whole
4 tablespoons vegetable oil
2 tablespoons fresh lime juice

1. Preheat broiler for 15 minutes or prepare the grill.
2. Season chicken lightly with salt and pepper, since the sauce will be spicy. Mix the oil and lime juice and brush the chicken and scallions with the mixture.
3. Broil or grill the scallions about 2 minutes on each side, breasts about 7 minutes on each side, thighs about 9 minutes on each side. While the chicken is cooking prepare the sauce.

EGG AND VINEGAR SAUCE

2 tablespoons unsalted butter
6 shallots, chopped
6 large mushrooms, thinly sliced
1 bunch cilantro, or Chinese parsley, stems and leaves separated
1½ jalapeño peppers (fresh or jarred), chopped with seeds
2 cups chicken stock (page 224) or canned chicken broth
1 cup heavy cream
3 egg yolks
3 tablespoons granulated sugar
¼ cup red wine vinegar

1. To make the sauce: Melt the butter in a medium-sized skillet over medium heat. Cook the shallots and mushrooms until soft, about 10 minutes. Add *cilantro* stems and *jala-*

How to Temper Egg Yolks

If a large amount of hot liquid is added directly to egg yolks, the yolks will coagulate. To avoid this, add a bit of the hot liquid into the egg yolks *before* combining the two mixtures. This is called tempering and is the key to creating a smooth, perfectly cooked sauce instead of scrambled eggs.

Once combined, cook over low heat. Never bring the sauce to a boil. Stir constantly.

peños; lower heat and cook for 5 minutes. Pour in the stock, turn heat to high and cook until the liquid in the pan is reduced by half. Pour in the cream and return to a boil. Remove from heat. Puree in blender or food processor and set aside.

2. In a small bowl, whisk together the egg yolks, sugar and vinegar. Pour one cup of the hot puree into the egg mixture to combine the hot and cold mixtures gradually. Then pour the pureed sauce and the egg mixture into the skillet and cook over low heat, stirring constantly, until thick and smooth.

3. To serve as they do at City Restaurant: Arrange two pieces of chicken on top of a bed of *basmati* rice. Top with the sauce. Garnish with fresh *cilantro* leaves and scallions and serve immediately.

Serves 4 to 6

Grilled Chicken with Tomatillo Sauce

Roy Yamaguchi of 385 North

The hot California summer inspired Roy Yamaguchi to create this cool Mexican-style barbecue. The *tomatillos* (which look like small green tomatoes with a husk), mix with the *cilantro* and lemon to create a cool base for the spicier tastes in the sauce. Bear in mind that the chicken should marinate for at least four hours, so leave enough time. On the other hand, this is a convenient dish for a couple to prepare—one can be outside grilling while the other is preparing the sauce. Serve at the end of a hot day with salad and cold beer.

4 half chicken breasts, boneless
4 chicken thighs, boneless

MARINADE

1 cup olive oil
2 bunches fresh cilantro, *chopped*
¼ cup fresh oregano, chopped
1 lemon, sliced

1. Combine the marinade ingredients in a large bowl, add chicken; cover and refrigerate at least 4 hours, although you can leave the chicken overnight.

2. Grill or broil the chicken 7 minutes on each side for breasts, 9 minutes on each side for thighs. While the chicken is grilling, prepare the sauce.

TOMATILLO SAUCE

2 tablespoons unsalted butter
¼ onion, chopped
¼ teaspoon ground coriander
½ teaspoon ground cumin
2 garlic cloves, crushed
½ jalapeño *pepper (fresh or jarred), chopped*
6 tomatillos, husks removed and chopped, or two 10-ounce cans, drained

Grilling Tips

When grilling outdoors it is ideal to use a combination of charcoal and wood, but exactly what combination is up to you. The best way to learn about the different coals and woods is by tasting food grilled on them.

Any wood that has been soaked in water for about two hours will add a smoky flavor to grilled foods. Hickory wood adds a sweet, smoky flavor that is especially delicious with beef and pork. Mesquite coal, which is popular with many California chefs, imparts a rich, clean, woody flavor to beef, chicken, pork and fish. Grapevine cuttings added to charcoal make a sweet complement to delicate fish and chicken grills. Try your own combinations but avoid using lighter fluid or commercial briquets that contain harmful chemicals.

To cook the *tomatillo* mixture, melt the butter in a 10-inch sauté pan over medium-low heat. Add the onion, coriander and cumin and sauté about 5 minutes, until the onion is soft. Add the garlic and *jalapeño*; cook for another minute. Add the *tomatillos* and cook over medium heat for 10 minutes. Puree the hot mixture in a food processor or blender. While the *tomatillo* mixture is cooking, prepare the *beurre blanc*.

BEURRE BLANC

¾ cup dry white wine
3 tablespoons white wine vinegar
2 small shallots, minced
2 tablespoons heavy cream
1 cup (2 sticks) unsalted butter, at room temperature

1. In another 10-inch sauté pan, cook the wine, vinegar and shallots over high heat until the liquid is reduced to a syrupy consistency.

2. Add the cream and continue to cook until reduced by half. Remove from heat.

3. Whisk in butter, one tablespoon at a time, making sure that each addition is completely melted before adding the next.

4. Pour the *tomatillo* mixture into the *beurre blanc* and strain. Coat each serving plate with the sauce and top with chicken. Serve immediately.

Serves 4

Duck Breast with Apples and Calvados

Jean-François Meteigner of L'Orangerie

Jean-François learned how to cook at some of the finest restaurants in France before coming to America at the age of twenty-two to become chef at L'Orangerie.

This classic dish of Normandy recalls dinners he prepared at three-star restaurants like Troisgros and L'Archestrate. Preparation time is surprisingly short, about twenty minutes, if you make the duck stock in advance. Jean-François suggests serving this elegant entrée with a baked potato or green beans. He recommends a bottle of red wine from Bordeaux.

1 medium duck

Remove the duck breasts; debone and trim excess skin. Thoroughly debone the duck and reserve legs for Grilled Duck Salad (page 84). Chop the carcass into 2-inch pieces. You can ask your butcher to debone the duck and reserve the carcass.

DUCK STOCK

Duck bones and carcass
2 tablespoons vegetable oil
1 large carrot, peeled and chopped
2 celery stalks, chopped
1 garlic clove, crushed and minced
1 onion, chopped
2 tablespoons calvados or other apple brandy
1 cup water

Heat the oil in a medium-sized skillet over medium-high heat. Cook the bones until well browned, about 10 minutes. Add the carrot, celery, garlic and onion; sauté for about 2 minutes. Add the calvados, scraping the bottom of the pan to release the brown bits. Pour in water, reduce heat to medium and cook, partially covered, for half an hour. Strain the stock and reserve. The stock, which will be the base for the sauce, may be made a day or two in advance and refrigerated.

Calvados

Calvados is an apple brandy distilled from the hard cider of Normandy. It's traditionally used to add flavor to poultry, game or pork dishes as well as to apple-flavored desserts. The American equivalent is applejack, which can always be used in place of calvados.

SAUCE

Duck stock
1 tablespoon heavy cream
4 tablespoons (½ stick) unsalted butter, at room temperature
salt and freshly ground pepper to taste

Warm the stock over low heat in a medium-sized skillet. Whisk in the cream and butter one tablespoon at a time, over low heat. Add salt and pepper to taste; remove from heat and reserve.

CARAMELIZED APPLES

2 tablespoons unsalted butter
2 Granny Smith apples, peeled, cored and chopped in ½-inch
  cubes
4 tablespoons granulated sugar
2 tablespoons calvados or other apple brandy

1. Preheat oven to 400°F.

2. In a medium-sized skillet, melt the butter over medium heat. Add sugar and sauté the apples about 2 minutes, until they are coated. Add the calvados and continue to cook until the apples caramelize to a golden brown, about 5 mintues.

3. To cook the duck breasts: Heat a medium-sized skillet with ovenproof handle over high heat. Place the duck breasts, skin side down first, in the skillet and cook for 2 minutes on each side. Transfer the pan to the oven and bake for 5 minutes.

4. When the duck is ready, remove skin and slice breasts across the grain, on the diagonal, in thin slices. Arrange the slices in a circle on each serving plate. Place the apples in the center and surround with the sauce. Serve immediately.

Serves 2

Honey and Cranberry Glazed Duck

Cecilia De Castro of Ma Cuisine

This burnished honey and cranberry glazed duck makes a beautiful centerpiece framed with sprigs of fresh rosemary or other greens. We like roast duck for holiday entertaining because it doesn't demand much last-minute attention and it always feels special.

2 (4- to 5-pound) ducks
1 teaspoon fresh rosemary, minced
1 teaspoon salt
1 teaspoon freshly ground pepper
2 celery stalks, diced
1 small onion, diced
1 medium tart apple, peeled, cored and diced
1 tablespoon fresh parsley, chopped
juice of ½ orange
¼ cup water

1. Preheat oven to 450°F.
2. Remove the neck, liver and giblets from the ducks' cavities. Trim excess fat and wing tips. Sprinkle inside and out with rosemary, salt and pepper.
3. Combine celery, onion, apple, parsley and orange juice in a mixing bowl. Toss to combine. Divide the mixture and loosely stuff the ducks' cavities.
4. Prick the ducks' skin all over with a fork. Place in a shallow roasting pan, breast side up. Add the water to the pan to prevent spattering.
5. Roast for 20 minutes at 450°F. Then reduce temperature to 350°F and roast an additional 45 minutes. While the ducks are roasting, make the glaze.
6. After 45 minutes, remove the ducks from the oven.

HONEY-CRANBERRY GLAZE

1 cup water
juice of ½ orange
½ cup granulated sugar
½ cup orange honey
1 pound cranberries, fresh or frozen
zest of 1 orange

Roasting Tips

Beginning the roasting process at a high temperature and then lowering it ensures a crisp, juicy bird. The high heat quickly browns the outside, while the lower temperature prevents the skin from burning and the meat from drying out. The goal in roasting poultry is to heat the inside thoroughly so the warmth radiates throughout the bones, baking from the inside out. The water in the bottom of the roasting pan serves two purposes—it prevents spatters and creates steam to keep the bird moist.

1. Combine the water, juice, sugar and honey in a medium saucepan. Bring to a boil and reduce to a simmer. Add the cranberries and cook until the skins pop, about 5 minutes.

2. Divide the mixture in half, reserving one part for the relish. Transfer the remaining mixture to a blender or food processor and puree.

3. In a saucepan, cook the puree with the orange zest over low heat, stirring constantly to avoid scorching, until the mixture is reduced to a syrupy consistency, about 5 minutes.

4. Drain water from the ducks' roasting pan and brush the breasts and legs with glaze. Return to oven for 10 minutes.

CRANBERRY RELISH

reserved honey-cranberry glaze
½ cup raisins
½ cup chopped walnuts

1. Combine the glaze, raisins and walnuts in a saucepan. Cook over medium heat until mixture is as thick as relish.

2. To serve: Arrange the ducks on a serving platter with steamed vegetables and fresh greens. Serve cranberry relish in a condiment bowl.

Serves 6

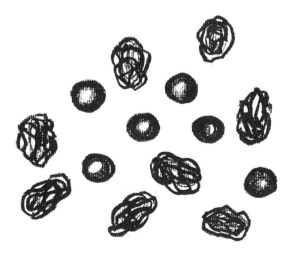

Szechuan Eggplant

Michael Kojima of Mon Kee

The inspiration for this complex combination of sweet and spicy tastes was the famous Chef Wong of the Imperial Hotel in Tokyo. It was in Mr. Wong's kitchen that Michael learned classic French, Japanese and Chinese cooking methods.

This is a recipe to tackle once you've mastered the shorter, less complex Chinese dishes. Although the list of ingredients looks daunting, most can be mixed in advance. All the Chinese ingredients are available at Oriental markets and some supermarkets. The Master Sauce, which is used with Veal Hunan (page 127), can be combined and kept in the refrigerator for up to 2 weeks. Use small Japanese eggplants, if available, for their sweeter taste.

2 ounces dry Chinese or shiitake mushrooms, soaked in warm
water for 30 minutes
1½ cups plus 2 tablespoons oil, peanut or soy
3 Japanese or 1 large eggplant, peeled and cut in ½ × 3-inch
pieces
3 ounces pork, thinly sliced and julienned
1 red bell pepper, stemmed, cored and julienned
2 canned bamboo shoots, julienned

SEASONINGS

1 teaspoon scallion, white and green parts, minced
½ teaspoon garlic, minced

SZECHUAN SAUCE

6 tablespoons Mon Kee Master Sauce (page 114)
1 tablespoon soy sauce
1 tablespoon granulated sugar
1 tablespoon rice wine vinegar
½ teaspoon Szechuan peppercorns

2 tablespoons cornstarch mixed with 2 tablespoons water
1 teaspoon sesame oil

1. Combine the seasonings and reserve. Combine the sauce

Step-by-Step Stir-fry

The key to anxiety-free stir-frying is organization. The cooking must be done quickly, so there's no time to fiddle around once the heat is on. For this reason we suggest chopping all the ingredients and combining the condiments for the sauce before the actual cooking begins.

Arrange the chopped ingredients in separate piles near the stove. Although you can stir-fry in a skillet, a wok is a good investment if you plan to cook Chinese food with any frequency. It is excellent for deep frying, steaming and stir-frying. Place the dry wok over high heat. When the wok is very hot, add the oil by pouring it in a circle near the rim so that it drips down and coats the sides and bottom. Heat the oil very hot before adding the ingredients in the order listed in the recipe. Usually, main ingredients like meat or seafood are first, followed by the seasonings, vegetables and sauce. The cornstarch mixture to bind the sauce is added last, often with a drizzle of sesame oil to add gloss and scent to the dish.

As you add the ingredients, constantly stir so that each piece is coated on all sides with oil and seared evenly by the heat. Use the time in the recipe as a guide but bear in mind that food should remain crisp and bright colored.

ingredients in a small bowl and reserve. Remove the stems and slice mushrooms in julienne strips and reserve.

2. Heat 1½ cups oil in wok over high heat until hot enough for deep frying. Add the eggplant slices and deep fry about 2 minutes on each side until golden. Remove with slotted spoon and set aside to drain on paper towels.

3. Drain the oil from the wok. Swirl in the remaining 2 tablespoons of oil and briefly stir-fry the seasoning mixture. Add the pork, red pepper, mushrooms and bamboo shoots. Stir-fry about 1 minute or until the pork is cooked.

4. Pour in the sauce mixture and cook an additional minute.

5. Return the eggplant to the wok and slowly add the cornstarch mixture. Stir until the sauce thickens.

6. Tip onto serving platter. Drizzle with sesame oil and serve immediately.

Serves 4 to 6

Mon Kee Master Sauce
Michael Kojima of Mon Kee

This all-purpose Chinese sauce may be mixed in advance and kept in the refrigerator for about two weeks. It's great for last-minute stir-fries as well as Veal Hunan (page 127), and Szechuan Eggplant (page 113). (Chinkiang vinegar is available at Chinese markets.)

10 tablespoons hot water
3 tablespoons soy sauce
2 tablespoons Chinese rice wine or sherry
2 tablespoons rice wine vinegar
1 tablespoon Chinese (Chinkiang) black vinegar (optional)
2 tablespoons granulated sugar
½ teaspoon freshly grated ginger
¼ teaspoon white pepper

Mix all the ingredients together in a small bowl.

Kick-Ass Chili

Leonard Schwartz of 72 Market Street

This chili really lives up to its name. It's thick and spicy—with no beans or thickener added. One taste will explain why homesick Texans make the trip to this Venice beach restaurant for a fortifying bowlful. Leonard serves his famous chili with the cornbread muffins (page 56) and with sour cream, chopped onion and shredded cheddar cheese as accompaniments. This chili deserves a large gathering of friends and you'll need a very large skillet and a very large stockpot to make it most efficiently. (You *could* cut the recipe down but it freezes well.)

½ pound thickly sliced or slab bacon, finely diced
2 large onions, chopped
2 tablespoons peanut oil
4 pounds center cut beef chuck, cut in ½-inch squares
2 pounds boneless pork butt or shoulder, cut in ½-inch squares
1 cup cold water
3½ cups ale
2 (32-ounce) cans pureed tomatoes
3 jalapeño peppers, seeded and finely diced
7½ tablespoons cumin
2 tablespoons dried oregano
2½ tablespoons cayenne
5 tablespoons pure chile powder
5 tablespoons New Mexican chile powder
1 tablespoon salt
2½ tablespoons garlic, minced
¼ cup fresh lime juice

1. Fry the bacon in a very large skillet until crisp. Add the onions; lower the heat and cook until the onions are translucent. Transfer to a very large stockpot and reserve.

2. Heat the peanut oil in the same skillet over medium-high heat. Add the beef and pork. Cook until the meat is brown, stirring occasionally. You will probably need to brown the meat in batches. Transfer each batch to the stockpot as it's browned.

Chile Powder vs. Chili Seasonings
When purchasing chile powder read the label carefully. The only ingredients in pure chile powder should be chiles that have been dried and ground. Packages labeled "chili seasonings" or "chili powder" usually contain other ingredients such as cumin, oregano and salt. If you're unable to find the hotter New Mexican chile powder that the recipe calls for, just substitute the same amount of pure chile powder.

3. When all the meat is browned, add the remaining ingredients except the lime juice to the stockpot. Stir well.

4. Turn the heat to high. Bring to a boil, reduce to a simmer and cook, uncovered, for 1½ to 2 hours, until the meat is tender. Skim off the oil that rises to the surface and stir the chili occasionally.

5. Stir in the lime juice and serve with your favorite accompaniments.

Serves 12

Marinated Sirloin with Gorgonzola Sauce

Susan Feniger and Mary Sue Milliken of City Restaurant

Impress the guests at your next barbecue with this special steak recipe. The sauce can be prepared just before you cook the steaks, but the meat must be marinated for at least six hours.

The hearty marinade, which is a Milliken family favorite, stands up well to the strong, distinctive flavors of the sauce. The chefs prefer Gorgonzola here to other blue cheeses for its creamier consistency and sweeter flavor. For more information on blue cheeses see page 78.

4 beef sirloins, about 10 ounces each

MARINADE

1 cup olive oil
2 tablespoons dry mustard
1 tablespoon Worcestershire sauce
1 teaspoon garlic, minced
1 teaspoon soy sauce
1 teaspoon fresh lemon juice
dash Tabasco
salt and freshly ground pepper to taste

1. Trim the steaks of all fat. Combine the marinade ingredients in a large glass or plastic container. Add the steaks, cover and refrigerate for at least 6 hours or overnight. Remove the meat from the refrigerator 2 hours before cooking to enhance flavors.

2. Grill or broil the steaks 5 minutes on each side. While the steaks are cooking, prepare the sauce.

GORGONZOLA SAUCE

6 shallots, finely minced
²/₃ cup Madeira
1½ cups veal stock (page 225) or canned beef broth
4 tablespoons (½ stick) unsalted butter, room temperature
4 to 6 ounces Gorgonzola cheese, crumbled

Fail-Safe Sauce Reductions

The purpose of reducing a sauce is to concentrate its flavor and thicken it through evaporation.

Always use a sauté pan or skillet (not a sauce pan) and medium-high heat. The more surface area exposed to the flame, the faster the sauce will reduce.

Don't stir the sauce while reducing. Stirring adds air, lowering the temperature and lengthening the reduction time.

1. To make the sauce: Combine the shallots and Madeira in a medium-sized skillet and cook over high heat until the wine is reduced by half. Add the veal stock and cook until the liquid in the pan is reduced by half. Remove from the heat. Whisk in the butter, 1 tablespoon at a time, making sure that each addition is completely melted before adding the next. Whisk in the cheese according to taste.

2. To serve: Slice the sirloins thinly, against the grain, and place on serving plates. Top with the warm sauce and serve immediately.

Serves 4

Sliced Fillet of Beef with Fresh Tomato and Basil Sauce

Celestino Drago of Celestino's

Celestino developed this quick, light beef dish for those who want to eat well without spending a lot of time in the kitchen. The beef is cooked very quickly in a small amount of oil with a smattering of tomato, garlic and basil. It's important to use the best quality beef, since it is so lightly cooked.

This is a great dish for entertaining after a busy day. Serve with grilled vegetables or a green salad and plenty of fresh, crusty bread to mop up the juices. Celestino suggests a light, red wine such as Dolcetto or Barbera to accompany this dish.

1 pound beef tenderloin
1 bunch fresh basil, stems removed
4 tablespoons olive oil
2 tablespoons water
4 garlic cloves, chopped
2 Italian plum tomatoes, peeled, seeded and julienned (page 101)
salt and freshly ground pepper to taste

1. Slice the beef against the grain in ¼-inch thick slices. Pound into ⅛-inch thickness and reserve.

2. Stack the basil leaves, roll in a tight cylinder and slice in ¼-inch strips.

3. In a medium-sized skillet, heat the oil and water over medium-high heat for approximately 1 minute. Cook the basil, garlic and tomato until the basil wilts, about 3 to 4 minutes. In the same skillet, add the beef and sauté briefly, about 1 minute on each side. It's important not to overcook the beef. Season to taste with salt and pepper and serve immediately.

Serves 4

How to Chiffonade

The method of slicing the basil leaves is called a *chiffonade*. It's the technique used by chefs to cut leafy lettuces and herbs into strips for salads and garnishes. Always remove and discard the stems. Stack the leaves, one on top of another, and roll lengthwise in a tight cylinder. Slice across the width in one-inch slices for salads and smaller widths for herbs. Fluff the strips with your fingers to separate.

Panfried Noodles with Beef and Vegetables

Michael Kojima of Mon Kee

Slicing Thinly

The key to slicing raw meat into the thin slices called for in this and other recipes is to chill the meat first to keep it firm. Place it in the freezer for about forty-five minutes and then slice it with your sharpest slicing knife or cleaver, always against the grain.

All over China and Japan, people love eating these crunchy noodle pancakes with assorted toppings, in much the same way that Americans enjoy pizza. Michael recommends using thin Cantonese egg noodles for the most authentic taste and texture, but you can also make the dish successfully with spaghettini noodles. Cabbage or lettuce can be substituted for *bok choy.*

1 pound thin Chinese noodles or spaghettini
5 tablespoons peanut or soybean oil
4 ounces beef, sliced in ¼-inch strips
4 bok choy stalks, green and white parts, sliced in 2-inch strips
2 ounces canned bamboo shoots, drained, sliced in 2-inch strips
2 ounces canned straw mushrooms, drained

SAUCE

1½ cups chicken stock (page 224) or canned broth
2 tablespoons Chinese rice wine
1 tablespoon soy sauce
1 tablespoon granulated sugar
1 teaspoon salt
2 tablespoons cornstarch mixed with 2 tablespoons water
1 teaspoon sesame oil

1. Cook the Chinese noodles according to the directions on the package. Drain and rinse with cold water.

2. Heat wok over high heat and swirl in 3 tablespoons oil to coat it. When the oil is hot add the cooked noodles. Fry for 5 minutes on each side, or until the noodles form a golden brown pancake. Tip the pancake onto a serving platter and reserve.

3. Combine the sauce ingredients in a small bowl and reserve.

4. Swirl the remaining oil into the wok and stir-fry the beef for 30 seconds. Add the *bok choy* and stir-fry 1 minute. Add the bamboo shoots and mushrooms; stir-fry an additional minute.

5. Pour in the sauce mixture and cook an additional 30 seconds. Add the cornstarch mixture; bring to a boil and continue to cook until the sauce thickens.

6. Tip the stir-fried mixture on top of the pancake. Drizzle with sesame oil and serve immediately.

Serves 6

Rib of Beef with Black Peppercorn Sauce

Jean-François Meteigner of L'Orangerie

How to Crack Peppercorns
Place the whole peppercorns in a dry, heavy skillet. Take another skillet, slightly smaller, and place it on top so that its bottom is touching the peppercorns. Press the skillets together and rotate to crack the peppers.

The classic combination of steak and black peppercorns is given a subtle interpretation by Jean-François. He suggests grilling over mesquite coals to further enhance the flavor of the beef and serving with Potatoes Gratin from L'Orangerie (page 168) and a selection of mustards, such as garlic, tarragon and green peppercorn. Jean-François suggests a heavy, red wine from Bordeaux to accompany this luxuriously rich entrée.

4 prime ribs of beef, 1½-inches thick, about 12 ounces each

MARINADE

4 teaspoons black peppercorns, cracked
1 cup olive oil
4 sprigs fresh thyme

1. For the marinade: Press ½ teaspoon of peppercorns on each side of each steak. Place the meat in a shallow baking dish; pour in olive oil and top each steak with a sprig of thyme. Marinate, covered, in the refrigerator for 24 hours. Remove the meat from the refrigerator 2 hours before cooking to enhance the flavors.

2. Grill or broil the steaks 8 minutes on each side, for medium rare. While the steaks are cooking, prepare the sauce.

BLACK PEPPERCORN SAUCE

8 tablespoons (1 stick) unsalted butter, room temperature
1 tablespoon black peppercorns, cracked
1 cup plus 1 tablespoon brandy
1½ cups veal stock (page 225) or canned beef broth
Salt to taste

1. To make the sauce: Melt 1 teaspoon of butter in a 10-inch sauté pan over low heat. Cook the peppercorns for 5 minutes. Add 1 cup of brandy, raise the heat to high and cook

for 1 minute, scraping the bottom of the pan to release the brown bits. Add the veal stock and cook until the liquid in the pan is reduced by half.

2. Remove from heat. Whisk in the remaining butter, one tablespoon at a time, until it is combined. Whisk in salt and the remaining tablespoon of brandy. Spoon the sauce on top of the steaks and serve immediately.

Serves 4

Veal with Apples in Port Wine Sauce

Cecilia De Castro of Ma Cuisine

Tender slices of veal in a rich port wine sauce are the centerpiece in this classic French presentation. The sautéed apples and endive, which can be prepared in advance and reheated, cut the richness of the sauce with a hint of sweet and sour. We suggest serving this entrée with a simple green vegetable and good French bread when the occasion is special.

2 heads Belgian endive
2 tablespoons unsalted butter

1. Preheat oven to 200°F.
2. Blanch the endives in boiling salted water for 5 minutes. Drain and rinse with cold water. Pat dry.
3. Slice each endive in half lengthwise.
4. Melt the butter in a medium skillet over medium heat. Place the endive in the skillet, cut side down and sauté until glazed and lightly brown, about 5 minutes. Turn over and sauté the other side for 1 minute. Transfer to an ovenproof platter and keep warm in the oven. Wipe the skillet clean with a paper towel.

VEAL AND APPLES

3 tablespoons unsalted butter
*2 large Delicious apples, peeled, cored and cut into 8 wedges
    each*
1 pound veal loin, cut into 8 slices
flour
salt and freshly ground pepper to taste
1 tablespoon safflower oil

1. In the same skillet, melt 2 tablespoons of the butter over medium heat. Sauté the apples, stirring occasionally, until golden and tender, about 5 minutes. Transfer the apples to the platter in the oven.
2. Lightly coat the veal with flour, and season with salt and pepper to taste. Melt the remaining butter with the oil over medium-high heat, in the same skillet. Sauté the veal for 1

minute per side. Transfer to the platter in the oven to keep warm, while making the sauce.

PORT WINE SAUCE

½ cup dry white wine
½ cup veal stock (page 225) or canned beef broth
¼ cup port
8 tablespoons (1 stick) unsalted butter, room temperature
salt and freshly ground pepper to taste
½ teaspoon fresh thyme leaves

1. Pour the wine, veal stock and port into the same skillet. Turn the heat to high, scraping the bottom of the pan to release the brown bits.

2. Bring to a boil and cook over high heat until the liquid in the pan is reduced by three quarters. Remove from heat.

3. Whisk in the butter, 1 tablespoon at a time, making sure that each addition is completely melted before adding the next. Season with salt and pepper. Whisk in the thyme and serve.

4. To serve: Place two veal slices in the center of each of four serving plates. Fan four apple slices on one side and an endive half on the other. Divide the sauce and spoon over the veal. Serve immediately.

Serves 4

Marinated Veal Chops

Evan Kleiman of Angeli

About Veal

Veal is the meat of a three- to fifteen-week-old baby calf. When properly cooked the meat is extremely tender and mild tasting. The best veal is labeled "milk-fed." Labels that read "Provimi" indicate that cattle has been fed additional proteins, vitamins and minerals. This does not ensure better tasting veal. The meat should be barely pink with very little fat. Unlike beef, there is no marbling. What fat there is should be white. Most recipes for veal in America call for scallops, which are the least expensive and quickest to cook. Veal is also available in chops (as called for in this recipe), ribs, breasts and shoulders for roasting, shanks for braising (see Osso Buco, page 129) and flanks for stewing.

Evan suggests serving this veal chop when you want something easy, yet extravagant. Ask your butcher to give you the loin chops with the fillet if possible, so that you'll have veal T-bone steaks, which are impressive and delicious.

The chops can marinate in the refrigerator for several days, if well covered with oil, to improve the flavor. It's important not to overcook the veal—the meat should be pink in the center. Evan suggests serving with some grilled seasonal vegetables or steamed asparagus and a light red wine.

4 (12-ounce) veal loin chops, 1½ to 2 inches thick
4 large garlic cloves, crushed
8 large sprigs fresh rosemary
1 cup olive oil
salt to taste
lemon wedges (garnish)

1. Place the garlic and half the rosemary in a baking dish. Lay the chops on top of the rosemary. Place the remaining rosemary on top of the chops. Cover with enough oil to coat the chops. Marinate in the refrigerator, covered, for a minimum of one day.

2. About an hour before serving, remove the chops from the refrigerator and wipe off the excess oil. Grill or broil the chops for 5 to 6 minutes on each side. Salt the meat after it's done, garnish with lemon wedges and serve immediately.

Serves 4

Veal Hunan Style

Michael Kojima of Mon Kee

For those who like their Chinese food hot and spicy, this dish deserves three stars. Michael suggests serving Veal Hunan with white rice, a red wine from Italy and a crisp green salad. You can control the heat by adjusting the number of crushed chiles in the sauce.

12 ounces veal, sliced across grain in ¼-inch thick slices
3 tablespoons oil, peanut or soybean

MARINADE

1 egg white
1 tablespoon cornstarch
¼ teaspoon salt

Combine the marinade ingredients in a bowl. Add the veal and let marinate for 1 hour at room temperature.

6 ounces asparagus, peeled, and sliced in 1-inch pieces diagonally
1 red bell pepper, stemmed, cored and cut in ¼-inch julienne
2 ounces canned straw mushrooms, drained
2 canned bamboo shoots, cut in ¼-inch julienne

SEASONINGS

½ tablespoon garlic, minced
½ tablespoon fresh ginger, minced
½ tablespoon scallion, white and green parts, minced

SAUCE

6 tablespoons Mon Kee Master Sauce (page 114)
5 to 10 chiles, crushed
2 teaspoons cornstarch, mixed with 2 teaspoons water
1 teaspoon sesame oil

1. While the meat is marinating, combine the seasoning

Michael Kojima on Chopping and Storing Vegetables

When we asked Michael, who was a *samurai* sword master in his native Japan, how important a specific cut is when chopping vegetables for Chinese cooking, he said the most important thing is keeping the shapes uniform within each dish. You can cut in julienne strips or dice or whatever shape you wish, as long as the shapes are the same.

Even better news is that much of the vegetable chopping can be done in advance. First, cut the vegetables and wash them in cold, running water for about fifteen minutes to make them crisper and remove any soil. Then dry them and store them in sealed containers in the refrigerator for up to twenty-four hours. They will remain crisp and fresh.

ingredients in a small bowl and reserve. Combine the sauce ingredients, adding the chiles according to taste, and reserve.

2. When the meat has marinated, heat the wok over high heat. Swirl in the oil to coat the wok. Add the asparagus and stir-fry for 3 minutes. Add the veal; stir-fry 1 minute. Add red pepper, mushrooms and bamboo shoots; stir-fry 1 minute.

3. Add the seasoning mixture and stir-fry an additional minute. Pour in the sauce and cornstarch mixture and cook until the sauce thickens. Tip onto serving platter and serve immediately.

Serves 6

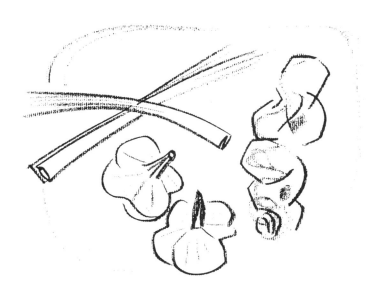

Osso Buco

Antonio Orlando of Valentino

While the menu at Valentino is changed often, some things just can't be improved upon. This classic Milanese recipe for braised veal shanks is one of them.

Chef Orlando suggests you ask the butcher to cut the shanks in pieces one and a half inches long and that you make sure the bones are included. When the veal is done, the meat should shrink so that half the bone is showing. The meat should be so soft and creamy that you can eat it Italian style, without a knife. Osso Buco, served with a *risotto* or a robust pasta and a glass of red wine, can take the edge off a wintry day.

On Braising

Braising is an excellent method of cooking inexpensive cuts of meat. The initial browning helps to heighten flavors and the slow covered cooking with liquid tenderizes the meat. It's important that the pot be thick and deep. Ideally, the meat should fit snugly. The lid should fit tightly so that the meat is steamed by the liquid in the pan.

2 ounces dry porcini mushrooms
8 veal shanks, cut in 1½-inch pieces
salt and freshly ground pepper to taste
1 cup all-purpose flour
4 tablespoons unsalted butter
4 tablespoons vegetable oil
1 onion, finely chopped
1 carrot, finely chopped
2 celery stalks, finely chopped
3 large tomatoes, fresh or canned, peeled, seeded and diced
2 tablespoons fresh rosemary, chopped, or 2 teaspoons dried
1½ cups dry red wine
¼ cup tomato paste
1 quart veal stock (page 225) or canned beef broth

1. Soak dry mushrooms in warm water to cover, until soft, about 10 minutes. Reserve the soaking liquid and mushrooms separately. Dry the mushrooms and chop finely.
2. Preheat oven to 350°F.
3. Season the veal with salt and pepper and dredge with flour. In a large skillet melt 2 tablespoons each of butter and oil over medium heat. Sauté the veal shanks until well browned on all sides. Transfer the veal to a large roasting pan.
4. Melt the remaining butter with the oil in the same skillet. Sauté the onion, carrot, celery, tomato and rosemary over medium-high heat, about 5 minutes. Add the mushrooms;

sauté for 2 minutes. Pour in the wine and cook until the liquid almost evaporates, about 5 minutes. Add the tomato paste, 1 cup of the liquid reserved from the mushrooms and veal stock. Stir to combine.

5. Pour the sauce over the veal and bake, covered, for about 2 to 2½ hours; until the meat falls off the bone. Transfer to a serving platter and serve immediately.

Serves 8

Lamb Tenderloin with Roquefort Sauce

Jean-Pierre Lemanissier of Ma Maison

Jean-Pierre learned the essence of *cuisine bourgeoise*—using the best ingredients to prepare traditional French cuisine—traveling the world as Paul Bocuse's *saucier*. Although he eventually stayed in California to become chef at L'Ermitage and then at Ma Maison, he remains faithful to Bocuse's philosophy.

This hearty lamb dish reflects those culinary principles well. The assertive tastes of lamb, garlic and Roquefort combine naturally in this elegant dish. The chef recommends a side dish of roasted potatoes and a red Burgundy wine.

1 tablespoon safflower oil
1 tablespoon unsalted butter
2 (12-ounce) lamb tenderloins, trimmed of all fat and bone

Heat the oil and butter in a large skillet, over medium-high heat. Sauté the lamb about 7 minutes per side, and keep warm while preparing the sauce.

ROQUEFORT SAUCE

1 tablespoon unsalted butter
3 shallots, minced
2 garlic cloves, minced
½ cup dry white wine
½ cup chicken stock (page 224) or canned chicken broth
1 cup heavy cream
¼ pound Roquefort cheese, crumbled
Freshly ground pepper

1. Melt the butter over medium heat in a 10-inch sauté pan. Cook the shallots and garlic until soft and translucent, about 4 minutes.

2. Pour in the wine and chicken stock, scraping the bottom of the pan to release the brown bits. Cook at medium-high heat until the liquid in the pan has reduced by half. Pour in the cream and reduce again by half.

Cooking with Cheese

Too much heat will make cheese grainy or stringy. Use only enough to melt the cheese and give the sauce a smooth, creamy texture. Always start with crumbled cheese at room temperature. Remove the pan from the heat and make sure the liquid is no longer boiling before whisking in the cheese. The warmth of the liquid in the pan should melt the cheese without overheating it.

3. Remove from heat and add the cheese, whisking until the cheese is melted and combined.

4. Transfer the sauce to a blender or food processor. Puree and then strain the sauce and adjust with pepper to taste.

5. To serve: Slice the lamb against the grain in ¼-inch slices and arrange on four serving plates. Divide the sauce; pour it over the meat and serve immediately.

Serves 4

Grilled Lamb Burgers with Zinfandel Sauce

Ed La Dou of Caioti

Ed puts his own twist on hamburger by combining ground lamb with the strong tastes of goat cheese, peppercorns and sweet red onion. The Zinfandel sauce is easy to prepare and provides a nice complement to the spicy meat. For an even quicker topping, serve each lamb burger with a dollop of butter or your favorite mustard. Ed suggests grilling some bell pepper slices and leeks to serve alongside these tasty burgers.

1 pound ground lamb
3 ounces goat cheese, mild preferred, crumbled
2 tablespoons chopped red onion
1 tablespoon fresh Italian parsley, stems removed and chopped
1 1/2 teaspoons canned green peppercorns, drained and crushed
1 teaspoon ground coriander
1 teaspoon salt
olive oil

1. Preheat the grill or broiler.
2. Combine all of the ingredients except the olive oil in a mixing bowl. Form into 4 patties and reserve.
3. Brush the patties with some olive oil before cooking. Grill or broil about 5 minutes on each side for medium-rare. While the burgers are grilling, prepare the sauce.

ZINFANDEL SAUCE

5 tablespoons unsalted butter
1 small shallot, minced
1/2 cup Zinfandel
1/4 cup heavy cream

1. Melt 3 tablespoons of butter in a medium skillet over medium heat. Add the shallots; sauté until brown. Add the wine; cook until the liquid is reduced by three fourths. Add the cream; cook until the liquid is reduced by half.
2. Remove from heat. Whisk in the remaining butter one tablespoon at a time. Top the burgers with the sauce and serve immediately.

Serves 4

Burger-Making Tips

Ed La Dou thinks that hamburgers, America's native food, deserve more attention than they've received from American chefs.

For the best burgers, pack the ground meat firmly into flat, round patties and refrigerate, if making in advance. When using ground beef, purchase meat with 15 to 20 percent fat content. The leanest beef does not make the best-tasting burgers. Grill, whenever possible, and when not, cook burgers in a very hot cast-iron skillet, without butter or oil. If the pan is hot enough, the fat from the meat will prevent it from sticking.

Roast Pork with Two Mustards and Sesame Seeds

Cecilia De Castro of Ma Cuisine

How to Toast
Sesame Seeds

In a small dry skillet, cook the
seeds over medium heat until
golden, about five minutes. Shake
the pan occasionally to brown the
seeds evenly.

This pork roast is great for weeknight entertaining. It's so fast and foolproof that Cecilia teaches it in her How to Boil Water class. Her only caution is that you resist the temptation to overcook the meat—half an hour should be just right. The roast can be served warm or at room temperature with a simple green salad or Cold Tossed Asparagus (page 162). Leftover pork, cut in julienned strips, makes a lively addition to Oriental style salads

1½ to 2 pounds pork loin, boned and trimmed
salt and freshly ground pepper to taste
1 teaspoon paprika
1 teaspoon dried thyme
½ cup sesame seeds, toasted
Dijon mustard
grainy mustard

1. Preheat oven to 450°F.
2. Season the pork with salt, pepper, paprika and thyme.
3. Place in a shallow pan and roast for 15 minutes. Lower the heat to 350°F and roast an additional 15 minutes. The meat should register 170°F on a meat thermometer. Set aside to cool before slicing.
4. Slice the pork thinly against the grain. Spread each slice with Dijon mustard so that half the slice is coated on both sides. Then dip that sauced half into sesame seeds to coat. Fan the slices in a circle on serving plates and serve with a scoop of grainy mustard in the center.

Serves 4 to 6

Grilled Quail with Confit of Onions*

Michael McCarty of Michael's

Michael's first venture into the food business in California was a partnership in a local poultry farm with the late Jean Bertranou of L'Ermitage. There they raised duck, quail and pheasant for southern California's growing restaurant business.

Quail is Michael's favorite game bird and it is hard to imagine a better complement to these crisp little birds than the rich bed of candied onions he calls *confit*. You can make this condiment, similar to a chutney, with any variety of sweet onion—Maui, Walla Walla or Vidalia, even red onions or shallots. Michael recommends serving this casual *bistro* dish with some good French fries and a bottle of Chardonnay. Please note that the quail must be marinated for at least a day before cooking.

12 quail, boned except leg bones

About Quail

You will probably have difficulty finding quail in the poultry section of your supermarket, so try ordering it from your butcher. Because it is so small, allow at least one bird per serving. The tender bones may be eaten.

MARINADE

1 cup olive oil
6 garlic cloves, crushed, with skins on
½ sweet onion, sliced
1 carrot, coarsely chopped
1 bunch parsley, stems removed and chopped
1 bunch fresh basil, stems removed and chopped
white pepper to taste

Combine all the marinade ingredients in a bowl or shallow dish. Add the quail and toss to coat the birds. Cover and refrigerate a minimum of 1 day or as long as 2 days.

CONFIT OF ONIONS

6 medium sweet onions, halved and thinly sliced
8 tablespoons (1 stick) unsalted butter, cut into tablespoon-sized pieces
salt and white pepper to taste

*From *Michael's Cookbook* by Michael McCarty.

1. Before grilling the quail, prepare the *confit* of onions. Pour a quarter inch of cold water into a 10-inch sauté pan with a tight-fitting lid. Add the onions, cover the pan and cook over medium heat for about 20 minutes, until the onions are translucent and no water is left in the pan.

2. With a wooden spoon, vigorously stir in the butter, one tablespoon at a time, until completely melted. Season to taste with salt and pepper. Reserve in a 250°F oven.

To prepare quail:

1. Preheat the grill or broiler

2. Season the quail with salt and pepper. Cook skin side down first until crisp and brown, 4 to 5 minutes; then flip birds over and cook about 1 minute more, until medium-rare. While the quail are cooking, prepare the butter sauce.

HERB BUTTER SAUCE

4 tablespoons (½ stick) unsalted butter
1 tablespoon fresh thyme leaves or 1 teaspoon dried
juice of ½ lemon
salt and freshly ground pepper to taste

1. In a small saucepan, melt the butter over medium heat. Stir in the thyme, lemon juice, salt and pepper to taste.

2. To serve: Divide the onions and arrange on six serving plates. Top each with two quail, spoon the herb butter sauce over the birds and serve immediately.

Serves 6

Stuffed Saddle of Rabbit with Mustard Sauce

Michel Blanchet of L'Ermitage

L'Ermitage serves only the very best of the classic French repertoire. This kind of cooking demands a great deal of time and patience, but the results are spectacular.

It is best to prepare the rabbit stock a day or two in advance. Chicken stock can be substituted for a less hearty flavor. The baked, stuffed rabbit can be prepared in advance and kept in the refrigerator for up to two days. Reheat in a 350°F oven until warm, while the sauce is reducing.

Michel suggests serving this dish with a hearty red wine, such as a California Pinot Noir or a French Burgundy.

4 saddles of rabbit (have a butcher remove and reserve the bones)

RABBIT STOCK

2 tablespoons unsalted butter
bones from the rabbits
1 onion, chopped
2 carrots, peeled and chopped
1 celery stalk, chopped
2 sprigs fresh thyme or ½ teaspoon dried
1 bay leaf
½ cup dry white wine

1. Melt the butter in a 10-inch sauté pan. Add the bones and brown them over medium heat. Add the onions, carrots, celery, thyme and bay leaf. Cook until the vegetables are brown, about 10 minutes.

2. Pour in the wine, scraping the pan to release the brown bits. Cook over high heat until the wine nearly evaporates.

3. Add water to cover; skim foam and cook at a simmer for 45 minutes. Strain, discarding bones and, if preparing in advance, store in a sealed container in the refrigerator.

BREAD STUFFING

4 slices toasted white bread, crusts removed
¼ cup heavy cream
¼ boneless, skinless chicken breast

About Rabbit

Rabbit is one of the most nutritionally perfect meats. It has more protein than chicken or beef, one third fewer calories than beef and a high potassium content. Because of its mild flavor it can easily be substituted for chicken, pork or veal.

You can purchase rabbit cut up in parts and frozen in the meat section of your supermarket, or fresh from your butcher. Try an Italian butcher shop if you're having difficulty, since rabbit is an integral part of Italian home cooking. The best tasting rabbits are about two months old and can be fried, sautéed, roasted or broiled. Older rabbits should be reserved for stews. It's best to marinate mature rabbits in oil and herbs before cooking to break down tough fibers.

1 ½ teaspoons chopped garlic
1 ½ teaspoons chopped shallot
1 ½ teaspoons fresh ginger, chopped
1 egg, cold
salt and freshly ground pepper to taste

1. Grind the toasted bread in a food processor or blender until fine crumbs are formed. Place the crumbs in a medium-sized skillet and the empty processor bowl in the freezer. Add the cream to the skillet and cook over low heat until the bread crumbs absorb the cream.

2. In the cold processor workbowl, combine the bread crumb mixture, chicken, garlic, shallot and ginger. Process with short pulses until finely chopped, about 15 pulses. Add the egg and process 10 seconds to combine. Season with salt and pepper; reserve.

3. Preheat oven to 450°F.

4. Place the rabbit saddles on a work counter and season with salt and pepper. Divide the stuffing into four parts and spoon it on each saddle. Roll; secure with string and transfer to a roasting pan.

5. Bake for 15 minutes. While the rabbit is roasting make the sauce.

MUSTARD SAUCE

2 cups rabbit stock
½ cup heavy cream
1 ½ tablespoons mustard
1 tablespoon fresh tarragon, chopped, or 1 teaspoon dried

1. Cook the stock in a large skillet over high heat until reduced by half. (Add tarragon if using dried herb.) Reduce the heat to medium, add cream and cook until the sauce thickens, about 5 minutes. Remove from heat and whisk in the mustard and fresh tarragon.

2. To serve: Divide the sauce and coat four serving plates. Place a stuffed rabbit saddle in the center and serve immediately.

Serves 4

Quick and Easy Bouillabaisse

Jean-François Meteigner of L'Orangerie

In his innovative recipe for *bouillabaisse*, the traditional fish stew of Marseilles, Jean-François has reduced the cooking time to an amazing thirty minutes. The key is making homemade fish stock in advance. Jean-François also has eliminated the customary bony fish. Any combination of skinless, boneless white fish will do as long as it totals three pounds. For a traditional French meal serve it over fresh garlic mayonnaise, with quantities of crusty country bread for dipping in the juices, and a fruit tart for dessert.

½ cup olive oil
1 onion, chopped
3 leeks, white part, cleaned and chopped (page 37)
3 garlic cloves, chopped
3 tomatoes, peeled, seeded and chopped (page 19)
2 cups fish stock (page 224)
3 sprigs fresh thyme
½ teaspoon saffron threads
1 pound large shrimp, with shell
1 pound skinless, boneless sea bass, sliced into 3 × 1-inch strips
1 pound skinless, boneless John Dory, sliced into 3 × 1-inch strips
1 pound skinless, boneless sole, sliced into 3 × 1-inch strips
½ pound cooked crab meat, cut into chunks
salt and freshly ground pepper to taste
Aioli Mayonnaise (page 228) (garnish)

1. In a Dutch oven or large saucepan, heat the oil over medium-high heat. Add the onion and leeks; cook until soft, about 5 minutes. Add the garlic and cook about 2 minutes; then add the tomatoes for an additional 5 minutes.

2. Add the fish stock, thyme and saffron; then simmer.

3. Add the shrimp, cook in the simmering broth, covered, for 2 minutes. Covering after each addition, add the sea bass, then the John Dory and sole, each for 1 minute. Remove from heat.

4. Stir in the crab, salt and pepper to taste. Serve immediately over a dollop of *aioli* in bowls.

Serves 8

The Best Way to Chop an Onion or Shallot

Since most chefs use this same method to chop an onion we assume it's the best. Once you master the technique we think you'll agree that it's the most efficient, causes the least eye irritation and results in the best flavor.

First, remove the skin. Cut the onion in half vertically and place it on a counter, cut side down. Holding the knife parallel to the board, make two to three horizontal slices from bottom to top, to within ¼-inch of the end. Then, holding the knife perpendicular to the board, make five to six lengthwise slices, depending on the size of the onion. Finally, slice the onion across all the cuts for a perfect dice.

John Dory in Tomato Herb Butter Sauce

Michel Blanchet of L'Ermitage

How to Thicken a Sauce with Butter

Mounting with butter is the most popular method of thickening contemporary sauces. Mastering this technique will enable you to prepare most of the elaborate dishes in this cookbook. The technique consists of two parts: first, the reduction of an acid-based liquid like wine; second, the addition of butter as a thickener. For a richer and more stable sauce, cream is sometimes added and reduced between the first and second steps.

The first step happens quickly, so stay nearby. Once the liquid is reduced, remove the pan from the heat and immediately whisk in the butter, one tablespoon at a time, making sure each addition is completely melted before adding the next. Always use unsalted butter and adjust seasonings with salt and pepper after the butter has been combined. The butter should be at room temperature when you start the sauce. If you find that your butter is too cold—if it doesn't melt while the pan is off the heat—return the pan to the stove and apply very low heat. If the heat is too high, the butter will melt too quickly, and separate. If the butter sauce does start separating, don't despair. Transfer the liquid to a food processor or blender. Puree, then add the remaining butter, cold, one tablespoon at a time. The sauce should become smooth again.

Many of the dishes at L'Ermitage are inspired by the cuisine of southern France, where the climate is similar to southern California's. In this fish dish, Michel takes the classic Mediterranean combination of white fish and fennel and enhances it with a subtle fresh herb sauce.

Plan an easy meal when serving this entrée, since it demands last-minute attention. Michel suggests serving it with a steamed green vegetable or potatoes and a dry, white wine, such as Chablis or Pouilly-Fuissé. Striped bass, red snapper or orange roughy may be substituted.

2 tablespoons olive oil
1 large fennel bulb, cut in half and thinly sliced

Heat the oil in a medium skillet over medium-high heat. Turn the heat to low, add the fennel and cook until soft, about 20 minutes, with the pan covered. Stir the fennel occasionally to cook it evenly. Keep warm in a 250°F oven.

TOMATO HERB BUTTER SAUCE

2 shallots, minced
1 cup dry white wine
2 tablespoons crushed tomatoes, canned or fresh
2 tablespoons fresh cilantro, or Chinese parsley, chopped
¾ cup (1½ sticks) unsalted butter, room temperature
1 teaspoon fresh chives, chopped
1 teaspoon fresh basil, chopped
1 teaspoon fresh parsley, chopped
1 teaspoon fresh tarragon, chopped
salt and freshly ground pepper to taste

1. Combine the shallots, wine, tomato and *cilantro* in a 10-inch sauté pan. Cook over high heat until the wine is reduced by half. Remove from heat. Whisk in the butter, one tablespoon at a time, making sure that each addition is completely melted before adding the next.

2. Puree the sauce in a food processor or blender. Add the fresh herbs and process briefly. Season with salt and pepper to taste.

4 (4-ounce) fillets of John Dory or other white fish
salt and freshly ground pepper to taste
1 tablespoon unsalted butter

1. Season the fillets with salt and pepper. Melt 1 tablespoon of butter in a 10-inch sauté pan. Sauté the fish 2 minutes on each side.
2. To serve: Divide the fennel and place in the center of four serving plates. Top with fillets, spoon on the sauce and serve immediately.

Serves 4

Seared Salmon with Herbed Corn and Red Butter Sauce

Roy Yamaguchi of 385 North

Cooking with Fresh
or Dry Herbs

A good general rule when
substituting dry herbs for fresh is to
use one third the quantity. Since
heat releases the flavor, fresh
herbs should be added near the
end of cooking time to keep the
flavors fresh. Add dry herbs at
the beginning to give them time
to reconstitute and release
more flavor.
Keep in mind that dry herbs
have a relatively short shelf life—
so buy small quantities and store
in a cool, dry place.

An exciting contrast of colors and textures marks this dish as distinctively Roy Yamaguchi's and also a great entrée for entertaining. Chef Yamaguchi suggests serving with a Pinot Noir or Burgundy. Red snapper may be substituted for the salmon.

HERBED CORN

8 tablespoons (1 stick) unsalted butter
2 ears of corn, kernels only
2 tablespoons fresh thyme, chopped, or 2 teaspoons dried
salt and freshly ground pepper to taste

Melt the butter in a 10-inch sauté pan over medium-low heat. Sauté the corn for 10 minutes. Sprinkle with fresh thyme, add salt and pepper and remove from heat. If using dried herbs, add the thyme 5 minutes earlier.

RED BUTTER SAUCE

1 cup red wine
½ cup white wine vinegar
3 shallots, finely chopped
3 tablespoons heavy cream
1 cup (2 sticks) unsalted butter, room temperature
salt and freshly ground pepper to taste

In a 10-inch sauté pan cook the wine, vinegar and shallots over medium-high heat until the liquid is reduced to a syrupy consistency. Add the cream and cook until reduced by two thirds. Remove from heat and whisk in the butter, one tablespoon at a time, making sure that each addition is completely melted before adding the next. Add salt and pepper to taste; strain and reserve.

4 (6-ounce) salmon fillets, ¼-inch thick
1 tablespoon unsalted butter

1. To cook the salmon: Melt the butter over high heat in a large skillet. Sear the salmon for about 1 minute on each side or until the edges turn opaque.

2. To serve: Divide the corn among the four serving plates and place in the middle of each plate. Place fish on top of the corn and pour the sauce in a circle around the outer edge of the plate. Serve immediately.

Serves 4

Salmon and Sea Bass Woven Navajo Style with Green Chile Butter Sauce

John Sedlar of St. Estephe

One of the benefits of keeping his restaurant small is that John has time to lavish attention on presentation. In this lightly baked fish entrée, strips of pink salmon and white bass are woven like an Indian rug and then placed on a bed of piquant green sauce.

Weaving the fish fillets is easier than it sounds. It's as simple as braiding hair. The fish strips are not delicate, so don't be concerned about their falling apart. This dish makes a striking entrée for entertaining. Serve with a steamed green vegetable or some boiled new potatoes.

1 (6-ounce) salmon fillet
1 (6-ounce) sea bass fillet
salt and freshly ground pepper to taste

1. Preheat oven to 375°F. Have ready a baking sheet lined with parchment or aluminum foil.
2. Slice each fillet against the grain into 8 strips, approximately ½ × 5 inches. To weave the strips, align four sea bass strips horizontally to form a square. Weave four salmon strips, one at a time, through the sea bass, forming a checkerboard pattern. Trim the edges with a sharp knife. Repeat the procedure with remaining fish to form two squares. Place on the prepared baking sheet and season with salt and pepper.
3. Wait until the sauce is reducing, and then put the fish in the oven to bake for approximately 6 minutes. It's not necessary to flip the fish while baking.

GREEN CHILE BUTTER SAUCE

½ cup white wine vinegar
1 tablespoon diced shallots
½ cup dry white wine
2 cups heavy cream
3 Anaheim or green chiles, canned or roasted, peeled, seeded and pureed
8 tablespoons (1 stick) unsalted butter, room temperature

1. To make the sauce: Combine the vinegar and shallots in a 10-inch sauté pan and cook over medium-high heat until the liquid is reduced by half. Add the wine and reduce the liquid again by half. Repeat the same procedure with the cream. After the cream has been reduced remove from the heat. Whisk in the pureed chiles and the butter, one tablespoon at a time, making sure that each addition is completely melted before adding the next. Strain the sauce, if desired.

2. To serve: Divide the sauce in half and coat two serving plates. Lift the woven fish squares with a spatula; place on top and serve immediately.

Serves 2

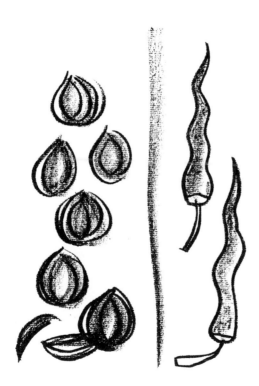

Poached Salmon in Tomato and Sorrel Sauce

Celestino Drago of Celestino's

On Sorrel

Celestino uses sorrel to flavor the salmon in this recipe for the same reason that lemon juice is usually added to fish—for its slightly tart, acidic flavor. Sorrel is a long, dark green leaf that resembles spinach but has a much sharper, more distinctive taste. Although this recipe could be made with spinach or basil, neither supplies the balance that sorrel does.

Although Celestino tries many different types of recipes at his restaurant—he changes the menu weekly—his favorite cooking is the simplest. This elegant, low-calorie fish entrée is a wonderful example of his style. The subtle blend of fresh tomatoes and sorrel complement the taste of the salmon without obscuring it.

Celestino suggests serving it with steamed vegetables and a dry, white wine. Remember, with this kind of quick, light cooking, the freshest ingredients produce the best results.

10 Italian plum tomatoes, peeled, seeded and pureed
$\frac{1}{4}$ cup dry white wine
3 tablespoons unsalted butter
6 (5-ounce) salmon fillets
2 bunches sorrel, stems removed and julienned
salt and freshly ground pepper to taste

1. Place the tomatoes, wine and butter in a large sauté pan with a fitted cover. Place the fillets on top. Sprinkle with sorrel, salt and pepper.

2. Cover the pan and simmer over low heat for 10 minutes. Serve immediately.

Serves 6

Fillet of Sole with Fresh Vegetable Sauce

Michael Feig of Country Fresh Herbs

In his class Fantastic Fish, Michael teaches his students about the flexibility and versatility of fish. Most fish can be steamed, baked, broiled or sautéed, and served with sauces varying from a classic *beurre blanc* (page 154) to a light tomato or vegetable, according to the cook's taste.

This colorful entrée, which he created at home with the ingredients at hand, is just such a flexible dish. Any boneless fish may be substituted for the sole. The vegetables may be changed according to the season (keeping color contrast in mind), and the sauce can be made even lighter by eliminating the butter and adding one cup of fish stock. Reduce the stock by half before adding the white wine. Then reduce the wine by half and serve Provence-style, in a soup bowl.

VEGETABLE SAUCE

1 cup (2 sticks) unsalted butter, room temperature
2 shallots, minced
2 garlic cloves, minced
1 red bell pepper, cored, seeded and julienned
1 zucchini, outer part only, cut into 2-inch lengths and julienned
1 yellow zucchini or crookneck squash, outer part only, julienned
2 scallions, white or green parts, julienned
5 mushrooms, cleaned and sliced
5 basil leaves, julienned
1 tomato, peeled, seeded and julienned (page 101)
½ cup dry white wine
salt and freshly ground pepper to taste

1. In a medium-sized skillet, melt 2 tablespoons of the butter over medium heat. Add the shallots and cook until translucent, about 2 minutes. Add the garlic and sauté 1 minute. Then add the vegetables in this order: the pepper for 1 minute, zucchini and squash 1 minute, scallion and mushrooms 3 minutes, basil and tomato 1 minute.

2. Pour in the wine and cook over high heat until the liquid is reduced by half. Remove from heat.

3. Whisk in the remaining butter, one tablespoon at a time,

Michael Feig on Purchasing and Storing Fish

For the best flavor, fish must be eaten fresh, preferably less than two days out of the water. Always buy fish from a busy fish market or supermarket on the same day you plan to cook it. Labels that read "fresh/frozen" are misleading. They mean that although the fish was once fresh, it was then frozen and defrosted before being placed on the counter for sale. It probably has very little taste left—to say nothing of the texture.

The eyes of whole fish should be clear and there should be bright red blood in the gills and inside the stomach. The signs of freshness in fillets are more subtle. They should not feel sticky and slimy and when you press the fillet, water should *not* rise to the surface. Fresh fish smells clean, not fishy.

Once home, fish should be kept in the refrigerator until cooking time. Never store fragile fish directly on ice. Place the fish on a perforated rack over a deeper pan. Cover the fish with a towel and surround with ice. Water from the melting ice should drain into the bottom pan and not come in contact with the fish.

making sure that each addition is melted before adding the next. It may be necessary to return the pan to very low heat to melt the butter. Keep in mind that this is a thin sauce, since there is no cream in the reduction. Season to taste with salt and pepper; reserve.

FILLET OF SOLE

4 (3-ounce) fillets of sole
salt and freshly ground pepper to taste
all-purpose flour
2 tablespoons safflower or vegetable oil

1. Season the fillets with salt and pepper. Dust lightly with flour.

2. In a medium-sized skillet, heat the oil over high heat. Add the fillets and sauté approximately 1 minute per side, until the edges are slightly brown.

3. Divide the sauce among four serving plates. Place a fillet on top of each and serve immediately.

Serves 4

Deep-Fried Scallops

Michael Kojima of Mon Kee

For the very best results, use extra large sea scallops when preparing this dish. When Michael cooks at home for friends, he enjoys mixing various ethnic cuisines. Since most Chinese dishes must be served quickly, try combining them on a menu with salads that can be made in advance, or soups that can be left on the stove to simmer while you're busy at the wok.

4 cups oil, peanut or soybean
12 ounces large sea scallops, muscle removed
cornstarch for dusting

1. Heat the oil in the wok over high heat until hot enough to deep fry. When a few drops of water are sprinkled in the oil, they should jump up.
2. Dust the scallops lightly with cornstarch. Place in wok and deep fry in two batches, about 1½ minutes each. Remove with a slotted spoon and drain on paper towel. Drain the oil from the wok and return it to high heat.

SAUCE

½ cup chicken stock (page 224) or canned broth
3 tablespoons soy sauce
1 tablespoon granulated sugar
2 tablespoons minced scallions, white and green parts
2 teaspoons fresh minced ginger
1 tablespoon cornstarch mixed with 1 tablespoon water

1. Combine the sauce ingredients in a small bowl.
2. Pour the sauce into the wok and slowly stir in the cornstarch mixture. Cook until the sauce thickens, about 1 minute.
3. Arrange the scallops on a serving platter; top with sauce and serve immediately.

Serves 4

Cornstarch in Chinese Cooking

The purpose of the cornstarch and water paste is to thicken the sauce so it clings lightly to the food. It's best to make the mixture right before you begin stir-frying, so the cornstarch doesn't completely settle to the bottom. Stir it again before adding to the wok, slowly drizzle it in and bring the mixture to a boil to thicken. When the sauce turns clear, within seconds, the dish is done.

Shrimp with Black Bean Sauce

Michael Kojima of Mon Kee

How to Peel and Devein Shrimp

Shrimp is sold according to the number of pieces to the pound. Medium shrimp are labeled U30, or under thirty shrimp to the pound. Large are U20 and Jumbo U12. Remember that by purchasing larger shrimp you're actually getting more meat in relation to shell in each pound.

To peel and devein: Pull the shell off with your fingers and discard. The intestinal vein runs along the back, not the inside, of the shrimp. Make a quarter-inch slice with a small knife along the center of the back, remove vein and rinse in cold water to remove any dirt.

Here's a familiar restaurant dish that's easy to prepare. Just clean and chop the ingredients, combine the sauce and stir-fry. Cooking time is about five minutes.

Once you've mastered the technique, Michael suggests using the same recipe to create a chicken dish by substituting chopped chicken breasts for the shrimp, and a green vegetable such as snow peas or asparagus for the pepper and onion. Scallops or oysters go equally well with the sauce. The black bean sauce and the Chinese rice wine are available at Oriental markets and at some supermarkets.

2 tablespoons peanut or soybean oil
1 garlic clove, crushed
1 pound medium shrimp, peeled, deveined and cut in half
1 green bell pepper, stemmed, cored and chopped in ½-inch dice
1 onion, chopped in ½-inch dice

BLACK BEAN SAUCE

1 tablespoon black bean sauce
¼ teaspoon chile flakes
1 tablespoon Chinese rice wine
½ cup chicken stock (page 224) or canned broth
2 tablespoons cornstarch mixed with 2 tablespoons of water
1 teaspoon sesame oil (page 93)

1. Combine the sauce ingredients in a small bowl and reserve.

2. Heat wok over high heat. Add the peanut oil and garlic; swirl to coat the wok.

3. Add the shrimp and stir-fry for 2 minutes. Add the onion and bell pepper. Stir-fry for about 1 minute.

4. Pour in the sauce mixture, stirring constantly, for about 30 seconds. Add the cornstarch mixture. Stir-fry an additional 30 seconds or until the sauce thickens.

5. Tip onto serving platter; drizzle with sesame oil and serve immediately.

Serves 4 to 6

Grilled Shrimp with Ancho Chiles

Bruce Marder of Rebecca's

Bruce was introduced to authentic Mexican cooking while working in the kitchen of the Beverly Hills Hotel. A Mexican chef there showed him the difference between what was being served at most southern California Mexican restaurants and real Mexican food. At his second restaurant, Rebecca's, Bruce serves the kind of food popular at restaurants throughout Mexico, like this beautiful shrimp dish.

Achiote, or annatto seeds, available at Latin American markets and the ethnic area of some supermarkets, lend color and a slight tomato taste to the oil. The seeds aren't hot and neither is the dish; chiles are used in moderation. At Rebecca's, Bruce surrounds the brilliant orange sauce with lime wedges and boiled new potatoes.

1 cup olive oil
2 tablespoons achiote or annatto seeds
10 garlic cloves, thinly sliced
2 dried ancho chiles, seeded and chopped
24 jumbo shrimp, with shells
olive oil for brushing
salt to taste

1. Preheat broiler or prepare the grill.
2. Combine the oil and seeds in a medium saucepan. Cook 2 to 3 minutes over medium heat until the oil is hot but not smoking. Strain the oil, discard the seeds, and return the oil to the pan.
3. Add the garlic and chiles and cook over low heat, until the garlic is soft but not brown, about 2 minutes. Reserve.
4. Wash and dry the shrimp. Butterfly with the shells on by slicing them open along the inside curve. Brush the shrimp lightly with oil, season with salt and place under the broiler, split side up, for 2 to 3 minutes. If grilling, place the shrimp split side down for the same time.
5. To serve: Place six shrimp on each serving plate. Divide the oil, spoon it over the shrimp and serve immediately.

Serves 4

Sautéed Shrimp with Mustard Sauce

Michael Feig of Country Fresh Herbs

Keeping Sauce Warm

In this recipe, the shrimp cooks so quickly the sauce will stay warm, but if you need to hold sauce warm for any length of time, you can place in a double boiler over gently simmering water, or inside an insulated carafe. If a delicate sauce must be reheated, place the pan over lowest heat and stir constantly until serving.

Michael's French grandmother taught him that food which pleases the eye stands a better chance of pleasing the stomach. This luxurious dish reflects her lesson well. The yellow in the mustard sauce creates a striking background for the pink-orange sautéed shrimp.

For a more casual presentation, Michael recommends serving the shrimp and sauce over a bed of pasta. All you need to complete a lovely dinner is a green salad and some cold, white wine.

MUSTARD SAUCE

8 tablespoons (1 stick) unsalted butter, room temperature
3 shallots, finely minced
5 mushrooms, cleaned and finely sliced
½ cup dry vermouth
1 cup heavy cream
2 tablespoons Dijon mustard
2 tablespoons grainy mustard
salt and freshly ground pepper to taste
1 bunch chives, minced (garnish)

1. In a 10-inch sauté pan, melt 2 tablespoons of the butter over medium-high heat. Add the shallots and mushrooms; cook until soft, not browned, about 5 minutes.

2. Add the vermouth; turn the heat to high and cook until the liquid is nearly evaporated. Pour in the cream and cook until the liquid is reduced by half. Remove from heat.

3. Whisk in the remaining butter, one tablespoon at a time, making sure that each addition is completely melted before adding the next.

4. After the butter is incorporated, pass the mixture through a medium strainer and return the sauce to the pan. Whisk in the two mustards. Season to taste with salt and pepper; reserve.

SAUTÉED SHRIMP

12 jumbo shrimp, peeled and deveined (page 150)
2 tablespoons olive oil
2 tablespoons unsalted butter

1. In a medium skillet, heat the oil and butter over medium-high heat until the butter is melted. Add the shrimp and sauté until just opaque, about 2 minutes per side.

2. To serve: Coat each of four serving plates with the sauce. Center three shrimp on each plate, garnish with fresh chives and serve immediately.

Serves 4

Grilled Marinated Tuna with Black Bean Sauce

Roy Yamaguchi of 385 North

How to Vary the Flavor of Beurre Blanc

Beurre blanc, or white butter sauce, serves as the basis for most classic French fish sauces. The key to varying its flavor is adding ingredients, like pungent black beans, after the basic sauce has been completed. Always add the flavorings immediately after the butter has been combined, and adjust with salt and pepper *after* the additions have been made.

Growing up in Japan, Roy spent every Sunday visiting the local markets with his father to see what was available for that evening's dinner. His father's enthusiasm for the freshest ingredients is reflected in this easily prepared, Asian-Western recipe. Swordfish or shark will blend equally well with the piquant sauce. Salted or fermented black beans are available at Oriental markets and some supermarkets.

4 (6-ounce) tuna fillets

MARINADE

½ cup soy sauce
1 teaspoon garlic, minced
2 teaspoons fresh ginger, minced
1 teaspoon granulated sugar

Combine the marinade ingredients in a large glass or ceramic bowl. Add tuna and marinate at room temperature for 10 minutes. While the fish is marinating, prepare the sauce.

BLACK BEAN SAUCE

1 teaspoon fermented black beans, rinsed and minced
1 teaspoon fresh chives, minced
1 teaspoon fresh ginger, grated
1 teaspoon fresh lime juice
1 tablespoon of the marinade
¾ cup dry white wine
3 tablespoons white wine vinegar
2 small shallots, minced
2 tablespoons heavy cream
1 cup (2 sticks) unsalted butter, room temperature

1. In a small bowl combine the black beans, chives, ginger, lime juice and 1 tablespoon of marinade. Reserve.

2. In a 10-inch sauté pan cook the wine, vinegar and shallots over high heat until the liquid is reduced to a syrupy consistency. Add the cream and continue to cook until the cream is reduced by half.

3. Remove from heat. Whisk in the butter, one tablespoon at a time, making sure that each addition is completely melted before adding the next. Whisk in the black bean mixture and reserve.

4. Grill or broil the tuna for about 2 minutes on each side.

5. Divide the sauce and spoon on four serving plates. Top with grilled fish and serve immediately.

Serves 4

VEGETABLES

Timbales of Broccoli, Cauliflower and Carrots

Jean-Pierre Lemanissier of Ma Maison

Cooking with a Bain Marie

By placing the timbales in a larger pan filled with water to bake, you are creating a *bain marie,* or water bath. Its purpose is to insulate the delicate mousse and keep it from browning on the bottom and sides. This is the traditional method for baking custards, bread pudding, pâtés and *mousselines.* You can use any pan with sides, as long as it is large enough to accommodate the mousse. First place the larger pan, empty, on the oven rack. Then put the timbales inside. Pour hot water into the pan, until it rises halfway up the sides of the cups.

These elegant individual portions of mousse can be served warm or chilled. For a special presentation, Jean-Pierre suggests filling each ramekin halfway and then adding bits of blanched, diced vegetables or precooked seafood before covering with the remaining mousse. You can substitute other vegetables, but aim for interesting color combinations. A six-cup terrine mold can be substituted for individual molds. Bake for one hour, slice thinly and serve as you would the individual timbales.

1¼ pounds carrots, peeled, cut in 1-inch pieces
12 ounces cauliflowerettes
12 ounces broccoli flowerettes
2¼ cups chicken stock (page 224) or canned chicken broth
2 tablespoons butter for coating
3 tablespoons unsalted butter
6 eggs
¾ cup heavy cream
salt and freshly ground pepper to taste
freshly grated nutmeg
sugar (optional)

1. Cook each vegetable separately with ¾ cup chicken stock in a saucepan with tight-fitting lid. Bring the stock to a boil, reduce to a simmer and cook with the lid on until each vegetable is soft. Approximate times: carrots, 15 minutes; cauliflower, 10 minutes; broccoli, 5 minutes.

2. Butter ten ½-cup ovenproof ramekins.

3. In a food processor, or blender, puree the cauliflower until smooth. Add 1 tablespoon butter, 2 eggs and ¼ cup cream. Process until combined. Season with salt, pepper and freshly grated nutmeg to taste. Divide the mixture evenly among the ramekins and set aside in refrigerator.

4. Repeat the same procedure with carrots, adding butter, eggs and cream in the same amount. Season with salt and sugar, if necessary. Divide the mixture and spoon over the cauliflower layer.

5. Repeat the procedure with broccoli, seasoning with salt, pepper and nutmeg. Divide the mixture and spoon on top of the carrot layer.

6. Preheat oven to 350°F.

7. Place buttered parchment paper or aluminum foil on top of the ramekins, touching the contents. Place the ramekins in a larger roasting pan. Carefully pour hot water into the pan until it is halfway up the sides of the molds.

8. Bake for 30 to 40 minutes. A knife inserted in the center should come out clean. Set aside to cool and then invert to serve.

Serves 10

Vegetable Fritters with Chick-Pea Batter

Susan Feniger and Mary Sue Milliken of City Restaurant

Some Tips on Deep Frying

Use a heavy, deep pan and
shortening, lard, vegetable or nut
oil for deep frying. Never use olive
oil, butter or margarine because
deep frying requires a high
temperature and the smoking
points of these fats are low.
Heat the oil to 350° to 375°F so
that the food being fried is sealed
immediately and no cooking oil is
absorbed. If your fritters seem
greasy, the oil needs to be hotter.
The best way to test the
temperature is with a deep fry
thermometer. If you don't have
one, drop a piece of food into the
hot oil. If the food immediately
rises to the top and bubbles form
around it, the oil is ready for
frying. Do *not* add more oil once
you begin frying.

Susan Feniger learned how to make these authentic Indian
fritters while visiting a family outside of Poona. You can substitute your favorite crunchy vegetables—cabbage and onion
are popular in India.

Chick-pea flour is available at Indian or Middle Eastern
markets. If you can't find it, make your own by grinding dry
garbanzo beans, a few at a time, in a blender or flour mill.

Try them at your next cocktail party with these sauces or
plain soy sauce, in place of the usual *crudités*.

BATTER

1 cup chick-pea flour, sifted
½ teaspoon ground turmeric
¼ teaspoon ground cumin
¼ teaspoon ground coriander
1 teaspoon whole mustard seeds
½ teaspoon poppy seeds
¼ teaspoon cayenne
¼ teaspoon baking powder
½ teaspoon cornstarch
¾ cup water
1 teaspoon vegetable oil
salt (optional)

3 cups vegetable oil
1 red bell pepper, stemmed, cored and sliced in ½-inch strips
6 medium-sized mushrooms, whole
1 cup broccoli flowerettes
2 cups cauliflowerettes

1. In a large mixing bowl combine all the dry ingredients.
Gradually mix in water until the batter thickens to the consis-
tency of heavy cream. Mix in the teaspoon of oil and reserve.
The batter may be made up to two hours in advance.

2. In a large saucepan, heat the 3 cups of oil over high heat
until extremely hot. Dip each vegetable piece in the batter to

coat and then deep fry for approximately 1 minute on each side, or until deep brown.

3. Remove with slotted spoon; drain on paper towels, add salt if desired and serve immediately.

Serves 4 to 6 as an appetizer
        about 30 pieces for hors d'oeuvres

SPICY YOGURT SAUCE

1 pint plain yogurt
¼ teaspoon salt
¼ teaspoon ground turmeric
½ teaspoon ground coriander
¼ teaspoon paprika
½ teaspoon Tabasco

Mix all ingredients and serve as dipping sauce.

Yields 2 cups

FRESH GREEN CHUTNEY

2 fresh ginger slices, about 2 inches × 1 inch
2 garlic cloves, peeled
2 bunches cilantro, or Chinese parsley, stems removed
1 bunch fresh mint, stems removed, or 1 teaspoon dried
1 large California or Anaheim green chile, cored, seeded and
   finely chopped
½ teaspoon salt
juice of 2 lemons
1 teaspoon olive oil

In a food processor combine and process ginger and garlic until finely minced. With the machine running, add *cilantro* and mint and process until finely minced. Add the remaining ingredients and puree until smooth.

Yields about 1 cup

Cold Tossed Asparagus

Renée Carisio of Ma Cuisine

Renée was inspired by visiting chef Barbara Tropp when she created this cold, light Oriental dish. Perfect warm weather food, this dish takes virtually no time to prepare, can be kept for days in the refrigerator and is easily packed for picnics.

1½ pounds asparagus, ends trimmed
zest of 1 orange, finely grated
1½ tablespoons granulated sugar
1 tablespoon soy sauce
1 tablespoon sesame oil
1 tablespoon dry sherry or Chinese rice wine

1. Slice the asparagus into 2-inch lengths. Blanch in a pan of simmering water until crisp-tender, about 4 minutes. Drain and refresh with cold water. Pat dry.
2. Mix the orange zest, sugar, soy sauce, sesame oil and dry sherry or rice wine together in a medium glass or ceramic bowl. Add the asparagus and toss to coat. Refrigerate 1 to 3 hours. Serve cold.

Serves 8

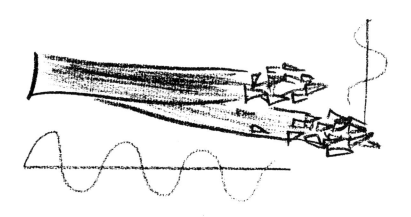

Cold Ratatouille

Linda Lloyd of Ma Cuisine

We like to keep this versatile dish on hand in the summertime. It complements a multitude of entrées, omelets, grilled meat, fish and roasts. Prepare at least an hour and a half in advance, to chill properly.

1 large eggplant, peeled and chopped in ½-inch cubes
2 teaspoons salt
3 tablespoons unsalted butter
3 tablespoons olive oil
3 garlic cloves, minced
½ medium onion, chopped
½ pound medium mushrooms, cut into ½-inch slices
3 medium tomatoes, peeled, seeded and diced (page 19)
1 teaspoon herbes de Provence (optional)
fresh lemon juice to taste
salt and freshly ground pepper to taste
grated Parmesan cheese (optional garnish)

How to Clean Mushrooms
Since mushrooms contain a lot of water and tend to absorb even more, we don't recommend washing them. Wipe mushrooms clean with a soft mushroom brush or damp paper towel. It is only necessary to peel when using as a garnish.

1. Place the eggplant in a colander. Sprinkle with salt and set aside for 30 minutes. Rinse and pat dry.

2. Heat the butter and olive oil in a medium skillet over medium heat until the butter melts. Sauté the garlic and onion until soft, about 4 minutes. Add the eggplant and mushrooms. Cook over medium heat, uncovered, stirring occasionally, for about 10 minutes. Add the tomatoes and *herbes de Provence*, if desired, and cook 10 minutes more.

3. Season with lemon juice, salt and pepper, and remove from heat. Set aside to cool and then refrigerate a minimum of an hour. Serve cold, dusted with Parmesan if desired.

Serves 6

Mushrooms with Fresh Asparagus

Michael Kojima of Mon Kee

Chinese Black Mushrooms

The Chinese black mushroom, or *shiitake*, is the most popular mushroom in Chinese cooking. Its spongy, plush texture makes it an excellent vehicle for sauces, and its rich flavor makes it a good main ingredient vegetable. *Shiitake* are available fresh or dry, but don't substitute one for the other in a recipe, because the dry version has a much more concentrated flavor. Dried mushrooms should be soaked in warm water for a minimum of thirty minutes, longer if possible. The stems are usually tough and should be discarded before proceeding with the recipe. Fresh and dry *shiitake* are widely available in the Oriental sections and produce sections of supermarkets, as well as at Oriental markets.

This is a good recipe for beginning Chinese cookery. There are only two ingredients to chop, and cooking time is about five minutes. Serve with a grilled or broiled fish entrée or steak.

2 tablespoons peanut or soybean oil
6 ounces dry shiitake, *or Chinese black mushrooms*
½ pound asparagus, peeled, and sliced in 1-inch pieces
*   diagonally*

SAUCE

3 ounces chicken stock (page 224) or canned broth
1 tablespoon sherry or Chinese rice wine (available at Chinese
*   markets)*
1 teaspoon salt
1 teaspoon granulated sugar
2 tablespoons cornstarch mixed with 2 tablespoons water
1 teaspoon sesame oil

1. Soak the mushrooms in warm water for 2 hours. Pat dry, remove stems and slice in ¼-inch strips.

2. Blanch the asparagus in rapidly boiling salted water for about 1 minute. Refresh with cold water, drain and reserve.

3. Combine the sauce ingredients in a small bowl and reserve.

4. Heat a wok over high heat. Swirl in the peanut oil to coat the wok.

5. Stir-fry the mushrooms and asparagus for approximately 1 minute. Pour in the sauce mixture, stirring constantly, for about 30 seconds. Add the cornstarch mixture. Stir-fry an additional minute or until sauce thickens.

6. Tip onto serving platter; drizzle with sesame oil and serve immediately.

Serves 4

Grilled Herbed Mushrooms in Cold Tomato Dressing

Cecilia De Castro of Ma Cuisine

Cecilia came up with this combination for actress Darryl Hannah, a vegetarian who cooks for meat eaters. The Philippines-inspired cold tomato and lime dressing is compatible with grilled fish or chicken as well as mushrooms. To prevent the bamboo skewers from splintering in the heat of the fire, soak them in cold water for about half an hour and place them in the freezer for a few minutes before cooking.

1 pound large button mushrooms, wiped clean

MARINADE

1 cup olive oil
4 garlic cloves, minced
1 teaspoon red pepper flakes, crushed
1 tablespoon fresh parsley, chopped
1 tablespoon fresh cilantro or basil, chopped
½ teaspoon salt
¼ teaspoon freshly ground pepper

Combine all the marinade ingredients in a glass or ceramic bowl. Add the mushrooms, toss to coat and set aside to marinate for 1 hour at room temperature.

COLD TOMATO DRESSING

3 tomatoes, peeled, seeded and chopped (page 19)
3 shallots, minced
¼ cup sherry wine vinegar
¼ cup tomato juice
¼ cup extra virgin olive oil
juice of 1 lime
2 tablespoons chopped fresh parsley
2 tablespoons chopped fresh cilantro or basil

Garlic

The easiest way to peel garlic is to crush the cloves with the side of a heavy knife or cleaver and then remove the skin with your fingers. You can use a small paring knife to mince. If you use a food processor, with the machine running drop the peeled cloves through the feed tube and process until finely minced. This technique is handy for mincing fresh ginger, shallots, and small quantities of herbs. By adding the ingredient with the machine running, you prevent it from sticking to the blade.

Combine all the ingredients in a bowl. Refrigerate a minimum of 1 hour or as long as 4.

1. Preheat broiler or prepare grill.

2. Divide the mushrooms among four skewers. Broil or grill 4 to 5 minutes per side.

3. To serve: Divide the cold tomato dressing among four serving plates. Top each with a skewer of mushrooms and serve.

Serves 4 as an appetizer or vegetable side dish

City Roasted Potatoes

Susan Feniger and Mary Sue Milliken of City Restaurant

The key to this dish is slicing the potatoes as thinly as possible
—almost like potato chips. Serve them alongside roasted
chicken or the marinated sirloin from City Restaurant (page
117).

3 large baking potatoes, peeled
¾ cup clarified butter
½ teaspoon salt
¼ teaspoon pepper

1. Preheat oven to 450°F. Have ready a large jelly roll pan
or baking sheet.

2. Slice potatoes very thinly across the width. Wash in a
bowl under cold running water for about 5 minutes or until
the water runs clear. Drain and pat dry with paper towels.

3. In a medium-sized mixing bowl, toss the potatoes with
the butter, salt and pepper to coat.

4. Randomly arrange the slices on the pan so that they overlap. Bake for 30 to 35 minutes or until the edges are golden.

5. Cut the thin cake into wedges or squares with a spatula
and serve immediately.

Serves 4

How to Clarify Butter

Clarifying butter removes the milk
solids and therefore allows you to
cook at higher temperatures.

To clarify the quantity called for
in City Roasted Potatoes, melt two
sticks of unsalted butter. Then
pour into a glass measuring cup
and refrigerate for about five
minutes. When the butter has
separated into layers of white and
yellow, remove from the
refrigerator and skim and discard
the foam from the top. Pour the
melted butter into a plastic
container, discarding the white
solids at the bottom of the cup.
Clarified butter can be kept
covered in the refrigerator for two
weeks.

Potatoes Gratin

Jean-François Meteigner of L'Orangerie

Types of Potatoes
When preparing a potato dish it's
important to use the specific type
called for in the recipe. The best
potatoes for baking and frying are
russet Burbanks, or Idahos,
because of their high starch
content. Red or white new
potatoes are delicious simply
boiled in their skins and served
with some melted butter and salt
and pepper. In California, yellow
Finnish potatoes are starting to
appear in some markets. They're
smaller than new potatoes with a
fuller flavor that's perfect for
boiling or making potato salad.
Potatoes should be stored in a
cool, dark place.

This potato dish develops a lovely brown crust on the top while the inside remains creamy and mild-tasting. It's best served with beef—like the Rib of Beef with Black Peppercorn Sauce (page 122) or your favorite roasted meat dish.

4 baking potatoes, peeled
3 garlic cloves, minced
½ teaspoon freshly grated nutmeg
1 cup heavy cream
½ teaspoon salt
¼ teaspoon pepper

1. Preheat oven to 350°F.
2. Slice the potatoes across the width in ⅛-inch slices.
3. Butter a 9 × 13-inch baking pan. Place half the potatoes on the bottom and sprinkle with half of the garlic and nutmeg. Add the remaining potatoes and top with the remaining garlic and nutmeg.
4. Bring the cream to a boil in a small saucepan and pour over the potatoes. Top with salt, pepper and additional nutmeg, if desired.
5. Bake for 50 to 60 minutes, until the potatoes are tender and lightly brown on top.

Serves 4

BRUNCH

Berries Supreme

Renée Carisio of Ma Cuisine

This eye-opener has been adapted from a recipe from the inventive Madeleine Kamman. The tart-sweet taste of berries is accentuated by marinating them overnight. We like to chill individual servings in wineglasses for luxurious morning meals or elegant picnics. Any extra strawberry sauce can be served over vanilla ice cream or Chocolate Tea Cake (page 184).

6 cups assorted berries, any combination
zest of 1 orange
¼ cup granulated sugar
2 cups strawberries, hulled and sliced
2 tablespoons Grand Marnier

1. Wash and dry the berries. If using strawberries, hull and slice them. Arrange the berries in a large serving bowl or individual bowls or glasses.

2. Combine the orange zest, sugar, strawberries and Grand Marnier in a food processor. Puree until smooth.

3. Pour the puree over the berries and refrigerate a minimum of three hours or as long as a day. Serve cold.

Serves 8 to 10

Smoked Chicken and Prune Sandwiches

Michael Roberts of Trumps

Try these rich little sandwiches when you need something special for an afternoon gathering. The leftover spread may be refrigerated and used for sandwiches and snacks during the week.

The inspiration for the liquor-soaked prunes in this recipe came from a college friend of Michael's who always kept a jar handy for snacks. The longer you let them soak the better. Michael recommends a minimum of a month, if you can wait that long. They're delicious plain or on top of vanilla ice cream for an easy dessert.

Why Unsalted Butter?

Since salt is added to smoked foods in the curing process, preparing the tea sandwiches with salted butter would result in *extremely* salty sandwiches.

Unsalted butter is always preferable for cooking. Since salt acts as a preservative, you have a better chance of purchasing fresh butter when salt has not been added. By cooking with unsalted butter and adjusting the seasonings yourself you can better control the amount of salt in your diet and the ultimate flavors.

½ pound pitted prunes
Southern Comfort or brandy
1 (2½-pound) smoked chicken
8 tablespoons (1 stick) unsalted butter, softened
½ loaf unsliced egg bread, crust removed

1. Place the prunes in a glass container to marinate. Add enough liquor to cover. Cover the container and refrigerate for a month, or longer. (Dried fruit marinades will keep in the refrigerator indefinitely.)

2. When it's time to make the sandwiches, puree the prunes in a food processor fitted with a metal blade. Reserve.

3. Remove the skin of the chicken and pull the meat from the bones. Puree the chicken meat in a food processor until smooth. Slice the butter in tablespoon-sized pieces and add to the pureed chicken. Process until smooth.

4. To assemble the sandwiches: Slice the half loaf of bread lengthwise into three slices. Spread the chicken mixture over the length of one side of the bread. Place another slice on top and spread it with the prune mixture. Top with the remaining slice and cut into small sandwiches, about one inch by two inches. Wrap in plastic and keep in the refrigerator until serving time.

Yields about 20 small sandwiches

Chicken Artichoke Turban

Renée Carisio of Ma Cuisine

Renée's Understanding *Phyllo* class always fills up early with students eager to learn how to work with the tricky, paper-thin Middle Eastern dough. She recommends this turban, cooked in a bundt or tube pan, for those intimidated by all the hand work of triangles. You can leave the turban in the pan for picnics or serve slices along with a green salad for a casual brunch or lunch at home.

2 tablespoons unsalted butter
1 large onion, chopped
2 chicken breasts, skinless, halved and cooked en papillote
1 (6-ounce) jar marinated artichoke bottoms, drained and
  chopped
12 ounces fontina cheese, grated
1 cup grated Parmesan cheese
4 scallions, white and green parts, chopped
4 eggs
1/2 cup heavy cream
3/4 teaspoon freshly grated nutmeg
1/2 teaspoon salt
1/4 teaspoon pepper
8 tablespoons (1 stick) unsalted butter, melted
1/2 pound phyllo, fresh or frozen
1/2 cup fine dry bread crumbs (page 204)

1. Melt the butter in a small skillet and sauté the onions until soft. Set aside to cool.

2. Chop the cooked chicken into 1-inch cubes.

3. In a large mixing bowl, combine the chicken, artichoke, fontina and Parmesan cheeses, scallions and cooled onions.

4. In another bowl, beat the eggs and cream together. Add the nutmeg, salt and pepper; whisk until combined. Pour the egg mixture into the chicken mixture and toss to combine. Set aside.

5. Preheat oven to 350°F.

6. Brush the bottom and sides of a 10-inch bundt or tube pan with the melted butter. Cut the *phyllo* sheets in half and

Cooking en Papillote

Baking en *papillote*, or in packages, is an excellent method for baking boneless chicken breasts (as well as fish and thin cuts of beef) for salads or for quick, light meals. For this recipe place chicken breast halves on a square of aluminum foil and fold the foil tightly to enclose the chicken. Place the package on a baking sheet and bake in a preheated 425°F oven for twelve minutes. By cooking the chicken quickly in a sealed package at high heat, the meat retains its moisture and delicacy.

layer them between pieces of waxed paper or parchment. Cover the sheets with a damp towel.

7. Line the tube pan by pressing the *phyllo* sheets inside the pan on a diagonal so they drape over the edges and overlap the top of the center tube. Each new sheet should overlap the previous one by half. Brush melted butter on the sheets before overlapping and sprinkle with bread crumbs. Circle the pan twice.

8. When all the sheets are lining the pan, fill with the chicken mixture. Cut an X in the *phyllo*, in the center where the pan's hole is, and fold the scored *phyllo* back, covering the filling. Fold the outside edges in, to seal the turban. Wherever *phyllo* overlaps, brush with butter and sprinkle with bread crumbs. When the filling is enclosed in *phyllo*, brush the top with butter and bake for 1 hour. The *phyllo* should turn golden and crisp. Set aside to cool in the pan for 15 minutes. Invert, slice into wedges and serve warm or at room temperature.

Serves 8

Green Chile Soufflés

John Sedlar of St. Estephe

Some Soufflé Tips

The base of the soufflé, which consists of béchamel sauce plus assorted flavorings, can be made several hours in advance and kept in the refrigerator until it's time to beat in the egg whites and bake.

The oven must be *very* hot to ensure a proper rising. Preheat the oven for at least ten to fifteen minutes, at 375° to 400° F, depending on the recipe. Make sure that the rack is in the lower third of the oven so there is plenty of air circulating above the soufflé to help it rise. Lastly, arrange the meal so that your guests are seated before the soufflé comes out. The life expectancy of the "puff" of the average soufflé is only a few minutes.

Jalapeño and red bell peppers combine with goat cheese for an unusually savory soufflé. Don't be concerned about the heat of the *jalapeños*—the hottest part is the seeds, which are removed. Only a hint of the fire remains.

At his restaurant John Sedlar serves this soufflé as an appetizer. We think it makes a wonderful centerpiece for a special breakfast or brunch, served with an array of fruit and some chilled Chardonnay. John suggests adding a tablespoonful of diced ham to the base if you use it for a morning menu.

2 tablespoons butter and flour for coating ramekins
1½ cups milk
6 tablespoons unsalted butter
4 tablespoons all-purpose flour
6 egg yolks, beaten
6 ounces goat cheese, crumbled
1 tablespoon red bell pepper, seeded and chopped
1 tablespoon jalapeño pepper, seeded and minced
½ teaspoon salt
½ teaspoon pepper
6 egg whites
pinch of cream of tartar

1. Preheat oven to 400°F. Butter and flour six 4-ounce ramekins.

2. Bring the milk to a boil in a small saucepan and remove from heat.

3. Melt the butter in a medium saucepan over low heat. Add the flour, whisking constantly, and cook for 2 minutes. Whisk in the milk; bring to a boil and remove from heat.

4. Add a small quantity of the hot milk to the egg yolks to gradually warm them. Then pour the egg yolks into the milk mixture. Whisk to combine.

5. Stir in the goat cheese, red pepper and *jalapeño*. Add salt and pepper; reserve. This is the soufflé's base and can be done hours ahead.

6. Just before assembling and baking, beat the egg whites with cream of tartar until soft, moist peaks form.

7. Whisk a third of the egg whites into the base mixture to lighten it. Gently fold in the remaining whites, being careful not to overmix.

8. Fill the ramekins to the top; level with a knife or spatula. Run your thumb along the inside to form a rim. Bake for 18 minutes or until the center wobbles slightly when jiggled. Serve immediately.

Serves 6

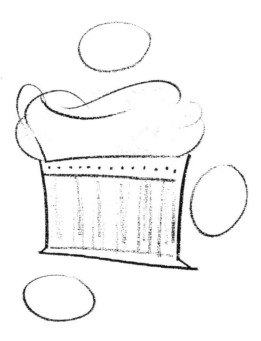

Grilled Lamb and Red Pepper Sandwiches

Bruce Marder of West Beach Café

Bruce's aim when he opened his own restaurant in 1977 was to create a neighborhood gathering place where his friends could meet for good conversation and fresh food. His West Beach Café, close to the beach in Venice, soon became known as one of the first restaurants to serve California Cuisine, which for Bruce meant cooking the kind of food he likes to eat at home. This sandwich, for instance, is good enough to serve when company is coming.

1 (12-ounce) piece of a leg of lamb
salt and freshly ground pepper to taste
1 loaf Italian or French country bread
4 red bell peppers, roasted and peeled (page 14)
1 Homemade Mayonnaise recipe (page 227) or prepared
  mayonnaise
1 tablespoon chopped fresh rosemary
8 ounces fresh mozzarella, thinly sliced
1 large red onion, thinly sliced
1 bunch arugula, washed and dried

1. Preheat broiler or grill.
2. With a very sharp knife slice the lamb off the bone in ¼-inch slices. Pound to flatten to ⅛ inch. Season to taste with salt and pepper. Grill or broil the meat about 30 seconds per side.
3. Slice the bread into ½-inch slices and lightly toast.
4. Handling the peppers carefully, slice off the tops and bottoms. Make one verticle slice, to open the peppers and remove the seeds.
5. Whisk the rosemary into the mayonnaise.
6. Make the sandwiches by spreading 8 slices of bread generously with mayonnaise. On 4 slices, layer the red pepper, followed by a slice of mozzarella, lamb slices, onion and *arugula*. Top with a slice of bread, cut and serve.

Serves 4

Home Fried Potatoes and Peppers

René Carisio of Ma Cuisine

This is the way fried potatoes were meant to be eaten in the morning—light and crisp, without a trace of grease. This large potato pancake with its slivers of bell pepper makes a colorful addition to a comforting meal of freshly squeezed orange juice, scrambled eggs and coffee. You might want to try frying smaller pancakes to serve as a vegetable side dish at dinner.

3 large baking potatoes, peeled and coarsely grated
3 bell peppers, any combination of red, yellow and green, cored, seeded and coarsely grated
1 teaspoon salt
½ teaspoon freshly ground pepper
2 tablespoons vegetable oil
2 tablespoons unsalted butter

1. Drain the potatoes of excess liquid and place in a large mixing bowl. Drain the peppers and toss together with the potatoes. Add salt and pepper; toss to combine.

2. Heat the oil and butter in a large skillet over medium heat. Spread half the potato-pepper mixture in the pan to form a large pancake. Cook until crisp, about 7 minutes each side. Repeat the same procedure with the remaining mixture, adding butter and oil if necessary, and serve immediately.

Serves 4 to 6

How to Flip a Large Pancake

The easiest way to flip a large pancake is to turn it over onto a serving platter, so the fried side is facing up. Then slide the pancake from the platter into the pan, so the uncooked side can fry.

Raspberry Almond French Toast

Renée Carisio of Ma Cuisine

In this upscale version of an American favorite, rich sand-wiches of raspberry jam and almond paste are gently sautéed in butter and then baked. Renée suggests making the almond paste, or *frangipane*, the evening before. In the morning you can make the sandwiches, sauté them and reserve them in a baking dish until the guests arrive. This is definitely a cham-pagne brunch dish!

4 brioches *or 16 small slices egg bread*
1 cup frangipane *(page 234)*
½ cup good quality raspberry preserves
3 eggs
3 egg yolks
¾ cup milk
½ teaspoon almond extract
2 tablespoons unsalted butter
confectioners' sugar (garnish)

1. Slice each *brioche* in 4 horizontal slices. Spread each of 8 slices of bread with a tablespoon of *frangipane*. Spread the remaining slices generously with raspberry preserves and make 8 sandwiches.

2. In a shallow baking dish, whisk together the eggs, egg yolk, milk and almond extract. Let the sandwiches soak in this mixture, turning occasionally, about 20 minutes.

3. Preheat oven to 350°F.

4. Melt the butter over low heat in a large skillet. Sauté the sandwiches about 3 minutes per side and transfer to a baking dish.

5. Bake about 10 minutes to melt the fillings. Dust with confectioners' sugar and serve immediately.

Serves 4

Homemade Breakfast Sausage

Renée Carisio of Ma Cuisine

Renée developed this recipe for purists like herself who enjoy a hearty breakfast but try to avoid the nitrates and preservatives found in prepared sausages. By making your own, you can control the amount of fat as well as the quality of meat in your sausage. Renée does, however, recommend a minimum of about one-third fat for proper taste and consistency.

You can slice the large log in this recipe into half-inch servings, wrap each in plastic and freeze them. To defrost, transfer the slices to the refrigerator overnight.

1½ pounds boneless pork shoulder
8 ounces pork fat
1 onion, quartered
1 cup fresh parsley, stems removed
½ teaspoon dried sage
½ teaspoon dried thyme
½ teaspoon dried oregano
¼ teaspoon cinnamon
¼ teaspoon nutmeg
1 teaspoon salt
¼ teaspoon freshly ground black pepper
¼ teaspoon Tabasco

1. Cut the pork and fat into ½-inch cubes. Reserve in the refrigerator.
2. Combine the onion and parsley in a food processor. Pulse until finely minced. Transfer to a bowl.
3. Place pork mixture in the workbowl and process until finely chopped. If your food processor is too small to accommodate the full amount, process in batches, being sure to combine the pork and fat in the same proportion each time.
4. When all the pork and fat are chopped, transfer to a mix-

Grinding Meat in the Food Processor

The food processor is ideal for grinding meat for hamburgers, pâtés or stuffings. Always chill the meat and fat the recipe calls for first, then cut into one-inch cubes and process with two-second pulses until ground to the consistency you prefer. If you need to work in batches, maintain the same proportion of fat to meat in each batch.

ing bowl and add the onion, parsley and remaining ingredients. Mix until combined.

5. Shape the mixture into a 12-inch long by 3-inch wide log. Wrap well with plastic wrap and refrigerate for 4 hours or freeze. It's important not to skip this step, since the flavors need time to develop.

6. To cook the sausages: Slice into ¼ to 1-inch-thick slices. Coat the patties lightly with flour and fry in a dry skillet over medium-high heat until golden, about 7 minutes per side.

Yields 10 to 12 patties

Lemon Waffles with Raspberry Sauce

Renée Carisio of Ma Cuisine

These waffles are prettier and more delicate than most. Lemon and buttermilk make them lighter; and the fresh raspberry sauce has none of the stickiness of prepared toppings. Renée likes to serve thin slices of Canadian bacon with the waffles and chilled cups of fruit salad.

About Buttermilk

Buttermilk's lower fat content and slightly sour flavor give baked goods a lighter taste and texture than milk or cream. If you run out of buttermilk you can substitute one cup less one tablespoon skim or whole milk mixed with one tablespoon white vinegar. Let stand at room temperature for twenty minutes, then add to your recipe.

LEMON WAFFLES

zest of 2 lemons
¼ cup granulated sugar
3 eggs
1½ cups buttermilk
8 tablespoons (1 stick) unsalted butter, melted
¼ cup fresh lemon juice
2 cups all-purpose flour
2 teaspoons baking powder
½ teaspoon baking soda
½ teaspoon salt

1. Combine the lemon zest and sugar in a food processor. Process until the zest is finely minced.

2. Add the eggs, buttermilk, melted butter and lemon juice. Process until combined, about 10 seconds.

3. Add flour, baking powder, baking soda and salt. Pulse about 4 times, just until the dry ingredients disappear. The batter should be slightly lumpy.

4. To make the waffles follow the manufacturer's instructions on your waffle iron. While the waffles are baking, make the sauce.

RASPBERRY SAUCE

2 pint baskets fresh raspberries or 2 (10-ounce) bags, frozen,
*   unsweetened*
1 cup granulated sugar
confectioners' sugar (garnish)

1. Combine the raspberries and granulated sugar in a small saucepan. Cook over low heat, stirring occasionally, until the sugar dissolves and the berries break down, about 5 minutes. Strain the sauce to remove seeds, if desired.

2. Spoon the sauce on top of the waffles, dust with confectioners' sugar and serve immediately.

Serves 6

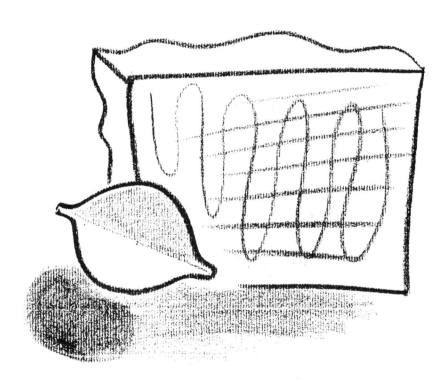

Pumpkin Waffles

Renée Carisio of Ma Cuisine

Renée was inspired by the cool weather on a recent trip to New York, when she created these rich, wintery waffles. They can be served with traditional maple syrup or topped with sour cream, honey, nuts and raisins for a special presentation. She recommends serving them with cinnamon flavored coffee or hot chocolate.

1 cup canned pumpkin puree
1 cup sour cream
1 cup milk
4 eggs, separated
8 tablespoons (1 stick) unsalted butter, melted
¼ cup packed dark brown sugar
1¾ cups all-purpose flour
2 teaspoons baking powder
½ teaspoon baking soda
½ teaspoon salt
¾ teaspoon cinnamon
¼ teaspoon freshly grated nutmeg
sour cream (garnish)
honey (garnish)
chopped pecans (garnish)
raisins (garnish)

1. Whisk together pumpkin, sour cream, milk, egg yolks, melted butter and brown sugar in a mixing bowl and reserve.

2. In another mixing bowl combine the flour, baking powder, baking soda, salt, cinnamon and nutmeg. By hand, stir the dry ingredients into the liquid, and reserve.

3. In a separate bowl, beat the egg whites until soft peaks form. Whisk one third of the beaten whites into the batter to lighten it. Then fold in the remaining whites.

4. To make the waffles, follow the manufacturer's instructions on your waffle iron. Serve with maple syrup or top each with a dollop of sour cream and a sprinkling of pecans, raisins and honey.

Serves 8

Chocolate Tea Cake

Michael Roberts of Trumps

A great recipe for the inexperienced baker. Michael Roberts's chocolate cake is fast, easy and delicious. The center is dense and moist like a brownie but the top, with its dusting of powdered sugar, makes for a much more elegant presentation.

The top is supposed to crack when you remove it from the oven. Don't be alarmed. The cake is inverted before serving. Michael suggests serving this with vanilla ice cream and a glass of milk, or with tea as he does at Trumps.

6 ounces semi-sweet chocolate, chopped
8 tablespoons (1 stick) unsalted butter, softened
⅔ cup granulated sugar
3 eggs
½ cup cake flour
confectioners' sugar

1. Preheat oven to 350° F. Butter and flour a 9-inch round cake pan and line the bottom with parchment paper.

2. Melt the chocolate in a double boiler or bowl over simmering water. Set aside to cool.

3. Cream the butter until light and fluffy. Gradually add the sugar, while continuing to beat. Pour in the chocolate and mix until combined.

4. Add the eggs, one at a time, beating well after each addition.

5. Gently mix the flour into the batter until it just disappears.

6. Spread the batter evenly in prepared pan and bake for 25 minutes, until cake tester inserted in the center comes out clean.

7. Cool cake in the pan, on a rack, for 30 minutes. Invert onto serving platter, peel the parchment and dust with confectioners' sugar.

Serves 6 to 8

About Cake Flour

Cake or pastry flour is available in the baking section of many supermarkets. It has the lowest gluten content of flours. Gluten, the protein component of grain, is what gives bread its chewiness. Cake flour, which is made from a softer wheat, produces a more tender crumb. If cake flour is unavailable in your area, you can substitute all-purpose flour by removing one tablespoon of flour per half cup and then sifting. This will soften the flour.

DESSERTS

Death by Chocolate

Patrick Jamon of Les Anges

This cake is guaranteed to satisfy the appetite of the most demanding chocolate lover—*and* it demands a lot of time, patience and rich ingredients. It is made of four contrasting chocolate parts—meringue, *génoise*, mousse and *ganache*—all prepared separately and then assembled into one very impressive cake.

Since he has been serving it every day for five years, Patrick has devised a few shortcuts. You can bake the meringue and *génoise* a day in advance and store them at room temperature, wrapped in aluminum foil, to keep out moisture. Start assembling the cake early on the day you plan to serve it, since it requires four and a half hours to chill properly. Or you can bake, assemble and freeze the cake with every layer but the final *ganache*. As soon as you take it out of the freezer, pour the warm *ganache* on top. This will result in an even glossier coating. One reward of mastering this cake recipe, aside from the obvious one of eating it, is that each part can be used individually. (See notes for ideas.)

CHOCOLATE MERINGUE

⅓ *cup egg whites (use about 2 large eggs)*
¾ *cup granulated sugar*
2 tablespoons unsweetened cocoa, sifted

1. Preheat oven to 250°F. Line a 10-inch springform pan with parchment paper.

2. In a double boiler or bowl over simmering water, combine egg whites and sugar until lukewarm, about 4 minutes. Remove from heat.

3. Beat the mixture with an electric mixer at medium speed until stiff peaks form, about 7 minutes.

4. Quickly fold in cocoa to prevent meringue from falling.

5. Using a pastry bag with ⅜-inch round tip, pipe the meringue in a spiral, starting in the center and working outward until the bottom of the pan is completely covered.

6. Bake for 2 hours. Set aside to cool in pan. Remove the pan, peel off the parchment paper and wrap the meringue in

aluminum foil or store in an airtight container. It will keep at room temperature for two days.

CHOCOLATE GÉNOISE

10 eggs, beaten
¾ cup granulated sugar
1½ cups plus 2 tablespoons all-purpose flour
2 tablespoons unsweetened cocoa
1 tablespoon butter, melted

1. Preheat oven to 350°F. Butter in a 10-inch springform pan, line with parchment paper and butter again.

2. In a double boiler, or bowl over simmering water, combine beaten eggs and sugar until lukewarm, about 5 minutes. Remove from heat.

3. Beat the warm mixture with a heavy duty electric mixer at high speed for 10 minutes, or until the batter forms a ribbon when the beaters are lifted. The batter should increase in volume by about four times.

4. Combine the flour and cocoa and then sift into batter in two stages. Fold until combined.

5. Whisk some of the batter into the warm butter. Then add the butter mixture to the batter and gently fold to combine.

6. Pour batter into the prepared pan and bake for 35 to 40 minutes or until cake springs back when lightly pressed. A cake tester inserted in the center should come out clean. Set aside to cool thoroughly in the pan and then remove. With a bread knife, slice the *génoise* horizontally into two layers ¼-inch thick, reserving the remaining cake for another use. Store the layers in a dry place, or wrap in plastic and refrigerate. The remaining cake may be frozen indefinitely.

CHOCOLATE MOUSSE

1 pound bittersweet chocolate, chopped
8 egg whites
½ cup granulated sugar
6 egg yolks

1. About two hours before assembling the cake, melt the chocolate in a double boiler or bowl over simmering water. Set aside to cool.

Ganache

Ganache is the easiest part to prepare and the most versatile. This simple cream and chocolate mixture can be poured warm on ice cream for a quick hot fudge sauce, chilled and whipped for cake frostings, spooned on a chilled cake for a glossy chocolate topping or chilled and rolled as a center for truffles.

Génoise

Génoise is the block upon which many classic French cakes are built. It is a dry cake that can be layered with butter cream, pastry cream, whipped cream, jelly or mousse. Pastry chefs usually sprinkle the dry layers with an alcohol and sugar syrup combination to keep them moist.

The crucial step in preparing *génoise* is the addition of the butter. It must be melted, and set aside to cool. To distribute the butter evenly throughout the cake, whisk about two tablespoons of the batter into the butter first. Then quickly fold the butter mixture into the batter, without overworking it. Baked *génoise* may be frozen indefinitely, stored at room temperature for a day; or stored in the refrigerator for several days.

2. Beat the egg whites until foamy. Gradually add the sugar, beating until stiff peaks form.

3. Add one third of the beaten egg white mixture to the chocolate and whisk until just combined. Add the egg yolks and whisk until smooth. Then gently fold in the remaining egg whites.

4. Refrigerate for an hour.

CHOCOLATE GANACHE

⅔ cup heavy cream
6 ounces bittersweet chocolate, chopped

1. After the mousse is chilled, bring the cream to a boil in the saucepan. Remove from heat.

2. Add the chocolate and whisk until the chocolate is melted. Reserve at room temperature.

To Assemble the Cake:

1. Place the meringue on the bottom of a 10-inch spring-form pan. Pour one third of the *ganache* on top and spread evenly to coat the meringue. Place a *génoise* layer on top. Spoon half the mousse over the *génoise*. Top with the second *génoise* slice and spoon the remaining mousse over the cake. Refrigerate at least 4 hours to set.

2. After the cake has chilled, spread the remaining *ganache* over the top and sides. Chill for half an hour before serving.

Serves 10 to 12

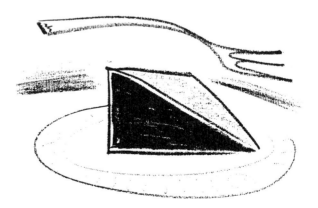

Spicy Pecan Layer Cake

Renée Carisio of Ma Cuisine

This classic American layer cake is an unrestrained celebration of a native American nut—the pecan. Both the cake and the butter cream frosting are generously packed with nuts and with liberal quantities of cinnamon and nutmeg. Though you can bake the cake layers in advance, the rich butter cream should be made just before assembling, for the best consistency.

8 tablespoons (1 stick) unsalted butter
1 cup granulated sugar
3 eggs, separated
1½ teaspoons vanilla extract
1 cup sour cream
2 cups cake flour (page 184)
2 teaspoons baking powder
½ teaspoon baking soda
2 tablespoons cinnamon
½ teaspoon freshly grated nutmeg
½ teaspoon ground cloves
¼ teaspoon salt
2 cups pecans, toasted (page 206) and roughly chopped
pinch of cream of tartar or ⅛ teaspoon vinegar

The Thread Test for Sugar Syrup

The first step in making this butter cream frosting is making a simple sugar syrup by cooking sugar with water. The best way to test the syrup for doneness is with a candy thermometer, which should register between 238° and 240°F. If you don't own a thermometer, you can drop a little of the hot syrup into a bowl of cold water. If a thread forms when you lift the sugar solution with a spoon, it is done.

1. Preheat oven to 350°F. Butter two 9-inch round cake pans and line with parchment paper, or grease and flour.

2. In a large mixing bowl, cream together the butter and sugar until light and fluffy. Add the egg yolks, one at a time, beating well after each addition.

3. Add the vanilla and beat until combined. Beat in the sour cream until combined.

4. In another bowl, sift together all the dry ingredients except the nuts and cream of tartar. Add to the liquid and beat until combined. Stir in the nuts and set aside.

5. In a metal bowl, vigorously beat the egg whites with a balloon whisk until frothy. Add a pinch of cream of tartar or vinegar and beat until stiff, but not dry, peaks form.

6. Whisk one third of the beaten whites into the batter to lighten it. Gently fold in the remaining whites.

189

7. Divide the batter and pour into the pans, spreading with a spatula to smooth. Bake for 30 minutes, or until a cake tester inserted in the center comes out clean. Set aside to cool in the pans, on racks, for ½ hour. Invert to release the layers and peel the parchment paper.

PECAN BUTTER CREAM FROSTING

1⅓ cups granulated sugar
1 cup water
4 egg yolks
1 pound unsalted butter, room temperature, cut in ½-inch slices
1 teaspoon vanilla extract
2 teaspoons cinnamon
½ teaspoon freshly grated nutmeg
1 cup pecans, toasted and finely chopped

1. Combine the sugar and water in a small saucepan. Bring to a boil and cook for 6 minutes, boiling constantly. The temperature should reach 238° to 240°F.

2. In an electric mixer with a wire whisk attachment, beat the egg yolks at high speed for 1 minute. Then gradually add the hot sugar syrup in a slow steady stream, beating constantly at high speed, until the mixture cools to room temperature, about 5 minutes.

3. With the machine running, add the butter, a little at a time, until combined.

4. Add the vanilla, cinnamon and nutmeg, beating until combined. Fold in the nuts.

5. To assemble: Place one cake layer on a cake platter and spread with one third of the frosting. Top with the second layer. Spread the remaining frosting over the top and sides. Refrigerate about 2 hours before serving to set.

Serves 8 to 10

Bizcochitos

John Sedlar of St. Estephe

John got this recipe for traditional New Mexican Christmas cookies from his grandmother, Eloisa, who lives in Santa Fe. He can remember watching her roll out the dough while she listened to high mass on the radio. At St. Estephe, John cuts the dough with cactus-shaped cutters, and serves the cookies with slices of fresh fruit and fruit purees. Any cookie cutter will do, of course. And if you don't have one, you can cut the dough into the shape of your choice with a sharp knife.

1½ cups granulated sugar
1 cup (2 sticks) unsalted butter, softened
2 eggs
1 teaspoon brandy
½ teaspoon vanilla extract
1½ cups all-purpose flour
1½ teaspoons anise seed
1 teaspoon baking powder
½ cup granulated sugar, for sprinkling
1½ teaspoons cinnamon, for sprinkling

1. Cream together the butter and sugar until light and fluffy. Beat in the eggs, brandy and vanilla until combined.

2. In another bowl, stir together the flour, anise seed and baking powder. Add the dry ingredients to the liquid and beat until combined.

3. Shape the dough into a one-inch-thick disk. Wrap in plastic wrap or waxed paper and refrigerate for 3 to 4 hours.

4. Preheat oven to 375°F. Line a baking sheet with parchment paper, or coat with butter.

5. Roll out the dough to quarter-inch thickness on a lightly floured board. Cut the dough with a cookie cutter or knife and liberally sprinkle each cookie with sugar and cinnamon. Place on the prepared sheet and bake for about 10 minutes, or until lightly browned.

Yields about 30 cookies

Chilling Doughs

Soft cookie doughs that are rich in butter require refrigeration before rolling. Chilling time can vary by recipe from as little as an hour to as long as overnight. Dough should always be firm to the touch before it is rolled. To roll, lightly flour the work surface, and work with half of the dough at a time. Try to work quickly so that the butter doesn't become soft. If the dough gets too soft or sticky, refrigerate until firm, and roll again.

Double Chocolate Brownies*

Michael McCarty of Michael's

These brownies are moist and chewy and intensely chocolate. And they're easy; all of the combining can be done by hand. At the restaurant they're served with a bowl of vanilla ice cream or on a cookie plate with *tuiles*, truffles, chocolate-dipped strawberries, macaroons and whatever else the pastry chef feels like baking—but they're terrific all by themselves, or with a cold glass of milk.

12 ounces bittersweet chocolate, best quality
3 tablespoons unsalted butter
¾ cup granulated sugar
3½ tablespoons water
2 eggs
¾ cup all-purpose flour
¾ teaspoon salt
2 cups walnuts, coarsely chopped
confectioners' sugar (garnish)

1. Roughly chop the chocolate into large chunks with a chef's knife.

2. Preheat oven to 325°F. Line a 9-inch square cake pan with parchment paper or coat with butter.

3. Combine half the chocolate with the butter, sugar and water in a medium saucepan. Cook over low heat, stirring occasionally with a wooden spoon, until the butter and chocolate have completely melted. Set aside to cool for 5 minutes.

4. Transfer the melted chocolate mixture to a large mixing bowl. Whisk in the eggs and then stir in the flour, salt and nuts until well combined. Stir in the remaining chocolate chunks until combined. The batter will be quite thick and lumpy.

5. Bake for 30 to 35 minutes, until a cake tester inserted in the center comes out clean and the sides pull away from the pan. Set aside to cool in the pan for 30 minutes. Garnish with confectioners' sugar, cut in 1½-inch squares and serve or store in an airtight container.

Yields 36 small brownies

*From *Michael's Cookbook* by Michael McCarty.

Tuiles

Patrick Jamon of Les Anges

Orange juice and Grand Marnier give these classic almond cookies their extra crispness. At the restaurant, Patrick fills the cookies with vanilla ice cream, fresh raspberries, a layer of *zabaglione* (page 221) and raspberry sauce. For a lighter version try serving *tuiles* filled with a scoop of sherbet or some fruit salad. The cookies will stay crisp for four to five hours if stored in a cookie tin or jar.

3 1/2 tablespoons unsalted butter
6 tablespoons all-purpose flour
1/2 cup granulated sugar
juice of 1 orange
1 tablespoon Grand Marnier
1 (2 1/2-ounce) bag sliced almonds

Tuiles Baking Tips

To bake these thin cookies evenly, turn the tray around when they're half done. When the *edges* turn brown, they're done. If they cool too quickly and become difficult to lift, return the tray to the oven for another minute or two to soften. We like to mold them against inverted bowls for the best cup shape, but you can drape them over a rolling pin for traditional *tuile* shapes, or the inside of a tube pan or anything small and round, like an orange, for example.

1. Preheat oven to 350°F. Have ready a cookie sheet lined with parchment paper and five small bowls for molding.

2. Melt the butter over medium heat until brown bits form at the bottom of the pan (see page 196 for tips on browning butter). Reserve.

3. In a mixing bowl, whisk the flour and sugar until combined. Add the orange juice, melted butter and Grand Marnier. Whisk until smooth and then whisk in the almonds.

4. Spoon a heaping teaspoon of the mixture on the prepared cookie sheet and spread with a small spatula, forming a thin, 3-inch wide circle. Repeat, making sure to leave lots of space between the circles since they'll spread. Bake each batch for 7 minutes.

5. Remove from oven and let the cookies cool on the trays *only* for about 2 minutes. (See note for baking and shaping.)

6. Working quickly, remove the cookies with a metal spatula and with your hands press them on top of small inverted bowls to mold. When they're crisp, in about a minute, remove. Serve immediately, or store in a cool, dry place.

Yields 10 *tuiles*

Hot Apple Tarts with Calvados

Jean-François Meteigner of L'Orangerie

It seems fitting that this recipe for individual puff pastry tarts with caramelized apples comes to Ma Cuisine from L'Orangerie, the most classic of French restaurants.

If you haven't the time to prepare the puff pastry at home, don't worry. Many supermarkets carry frozen puff pastry. Just defrost it before using. Serve tarts with sweetened whipped cream or vanilla ice cream.

1 Puff Pastry recipe (page 232) or 1 pound of packaged dough
8 tablespoons (1 stick) unsalted butter
6 Granny Smith apples, peeled, cored and thinly sliced
½ cup granulated sugar
2 tablespoons calvados, or any other apple brandy

1. Preheat oven to 400°F.
2. Melt the butter in a large saucepan over medium-high heat. Cook the apples and sugar in the butter for about 10 minutes, stirring frequently, until apples are soft and golden.
3. Puree half the apple slices with calvados in a blender or food processor. Place in the refrigerator with the remaining slices for ½ hour.
4. Roll out the puff pastry to ¼-inch thickness. Cut into six 4-inch circles and place on two large unbuttered baking sheets, allowing plenty of space between tarts. Spoon the apple puree on the center of each tart, spreading it within half an inch of the edge. Fan the apple slices on top of the puree, being careful not to drip the puree over the pastry shell. This would keep the pastry from rising.
5. Bake for 35 to 40 minutes, until pastry is puffed and well browned. Serve immediately.

Serves 6

Puff Pastry

Puff pastry is so delicate that exposure to the slightest heat before baking inhibits its ability to rise to its famous heights. Add only cold ingredients to the pastry and refrigerate the dough if it seems to be getting warm. It's the combination of cold dough and a very hot oven that results in the thin layers of butter and dough properly separating and rising.

Tarte Tatin

Cecilia De Castro of Ma Cuisine

This is a simplified version of the famous upside-down apple tart of Normandy. By reducing the size of the apple slices, Cecilia eliminates the need to stand by the stove adding slices as they cook down. Just crowd the slices into the pan, roll out the dough while the apples are cooking, and within an hour it's ready for the oven. Serve warm with a scoop of vanilla ice cream or fresh whipped cream.

8 tablespoons (1 stick) unsalted butter
1 cup granulated sugar
12 Red Delicious apples, peeled, cored and cut into 8 wedges
* each*
½ pound Puff Pastry (page 232) or Pâte Brisée (page 231)

1. Combine the butter and sugar in a 10-inch sauté pan with ovenproof handle. Cook over medium heat until the butter melts, about 4 minutes. Remove from heat.

2. Arrange a layer of apple slices on the bottom of the pan in a spiral pattern. Place the remaining slices on top in a circular pattern. The pan will be crowded when you start cooking, but the apples will shrink as they cook. Cook over medium heat, uncovered, about 1 hour, or until the apples start to caramelize. Remove from heat.

3. Preheat oven to 375°F.

4. While the apples are cooking, roll the pastry into a 12-inch round that is ⅛-inch thick. Prick all over with a fork and refrigerate until the apples are done.

5. Place the pastry circle on top of the apples, tucking the excess into the pan so that it encloses the apples. Bake 25 minutes, or until the crust is golden brown. Set aside to cool in the pan about 20 minutes. Carefully invert on a platter. If the tart doesn't release easily, return the pan to the stove and cook over medium heat 2 to 3 minutes to loosen sugar under the apples.

Serves 8

Cooking with Apples

Since *Tarte Tatin* cooks for a long time, we recommend using sweet Red Delicious or tart Granny Smith, because they remain firm for as long as two hours. For pies, where you want the apples to break down and soften, try Golden Delicious, Pippin or McIntosh. In recipes that call for sautéed apples (Potato Pancakes with Goat Cheese and Apples (page 17) or Duck Breast with Apples and Calvados (page 109) we recommend Granny Smith, because we like their tart taste. But if you prefer a sweeter apple, Red Delicious will do just fine.

Brown Butter Blueberry Tart

Roy Yamaguchi of 385 North

We like to make this extraordinarily good fruit tart in the summertime when fresh blueberries are plentiful, but if the summer seems too long to wait, you can use berries that are flash frozen, without any syrup. Don't thaw the berries, since they'll defrost during baking.

1 Pâte Sucrée *recipe (page 230)*

FILLING

¾ cup (1½ sticks) unsalted butter
3 eggs
1¼ cups granulated sugar
6 tablespoons all-purpose flour
1 tablespoon vanilla extract
2 cups fresh or frozen (unthawed) blueberries
½ cup toasted sliced almonds (page 206)
confectioners' sugar (garnish)

Browning Butter

Browned butter, or *beurre noisette*, gives food a rich, nutty flavor. Use a light-colored saucepan so you can more easily see the butter's color. Melt over medium heat until brown bits form on the bottom of the pan. By tilting the pan, you can easily see the bits. The key is to get them as brown as possible without burning.

1. Preheat oven to 350°F. Prepare the *pâte sucrée.*
2. To make the filling: Melt the butter over medium heat until a brown sediment forms at the bottom of the pan, about 3 minutes. Set aside to cool.
3. Combine eggs, sugar and flour in a food processor. Process until smooth, about 5 seconds. Pour in warm butter and process briefly until combined. Add vanilla, process 5 seconds and set aside.
4. Roll out *pâte sucrée* on a lightly floured board and use it to line a 10-inch tart pan with removable bottom (page 230). Place the blueberries and almonds in the tart shell; pour in filling and bake for 50 minutes to 1 hour, or until well browned. Cool on a cake rack. Dust with confectioners' sugar and serve warm.

Serves 8

Lemon Tart

Cecilia De Castro of Ma Cuisine

Cecilia teaches this cold lemon tart in her Basics II class to give her students custard-making techniques and a wonderful dessert recipe to take home. Lemon custard, or curd, is extremely versatile. It can be used for a tart shell or miniatures, spread on scones or toast at tea or served as an easy summer dessert in a bowl topped with berries. Store leftover custard in the refrigerator up to five days.

1 Pâte Sucrée recipe (page 230)

Preheat oven to 400°F. Roll out the *pâte sucrée* and line a 10-inch tart pan with removable bottom. Refrigerate ½ hour. Bake the empty tart shell with weights for 10 minutes. Remove weights and bake an additional 10 minutes. Set aside to cool. (See page 231 for additional information on baking blind, that is, without a filling.)

LEMON CUSTARD

4 eggs
4 egg yolks
juice of 4 medium lemons
juice of 1 medium lime
¾ cup granulated sugar
zest of 2 lemons, finely grated
6 tablespoons unsalted butter, cold, cut in tablespoon-sized pieces

1. Whisk eggs and egg yolks together in a large mixing bowl. Add all ingredients except butter. Whisk until well combined.
2. Place the bowl over a pan of simmering water, so the bottom of the bowl is not touching the water. Gently whisk until the mixture turns thick and creamy, about 10 minutes.
3. Whisk in the butter, one tablespoon at a time, until combined. Remove from heat. Cover with a layer of plastic wrap

Cold Pies or Tarts

To prevent a soggy crust, make sure your tart shell is at room temperature and the filling is well chilled before assembling. The tart shell can be baked as much as a day in advance and kept at room temperature. If either part is warm, the pastry will absorb the filling and soften.

touching the custard, to prevent a film from forming. Refrigerate 1 to 2 hours.

4. Pour the chilled lemon custard into the baked tart shell and refrigerate 2 to 3 hours before serving. Garnish with fresh raspberries or a layer of meringue.

Serves 8

Mincemeat

Renée Carisio of Ma Cuisine

Although most commercial mincemeat no longer contains meat, it was an integral part of this recipe when Renée's grandmother learned it as a young Colorado farm wife. Renée passes along this family recipe each year in her popular holiday gift-giving class. This full-bodied mincemeat makes a lovely gift sealed in jars or baked into holiday tarts, pies and cookies. Sealed in plastic containers it may be stored in the refrigerator up to two weeks or frozen about a year.

2 pounds boneless pork shoulder or Boston butt boneless
2½ cups raisins
1⅔ cups golden raisins
⅔ cup currants
6 Granny Smith apples, peeled, cored and quartered
1½ large oranges, with peel, cut into eighths
1 pound dark brown sugar
3 cups apple cider
1 tablespoon cinnamon
1½ teaspoons salt
1½ teaspoons freshly grated nutmeg
1½ teaspoons dried ginger
1½ teaspoons ground cloves
¾ cup brandy

1. Chop the pork in 1-inch cubes.
2. Combine the pork, raisins, currants, apples and oranges in a large bowl. Mix well.
3. In a food grinder or in batches in a food processor, finely chop the mixture.
4. Place in a large stockpot. Stir in the brown sugar, cider, cinnamon, salt, nutmeg, ginger and cloves. Cook uncovered over low heat, stirring occasionally, about half an hour.
5. Remove from heat. Stir in the brandy and seal in gift jars immediately or set aside to cool and store in plastic containers in the refrigerator or freezer.

Yields 8 cups

Pineapple Tart with White Chocolate Mousse

Jean-François Meteigner of L'Orangerie

Jean-François developed this recipe for Ma Cuisine as a way to combine two of his favorite flavors—white chocolate and pineapple. The cold mousse is piled very high, then topped with a glorious crown of thinly cut pineapple slices for a truly sensational looking dessert. This cold tart could be the perfect ending to a summer party. (But please note that it needs to be chilled for five to seven hours before serving.)

1 Pâte Sucrée recipe (page 230)

Preheat oven to 350°F. Roll out the *pâte sucrée* and line a 10-inch tart pan with removable bottom. Refrigerate 15 minutes. Bake the empty tart shell, topped with pie weights, for 10 minutes. Remove pie weights and bake for an additional 15 minutes. Set aside to cool. See page 231 for more information on baking blind.

½ pineapple, cut lengthwise and peeled
1 tablespoon granulated sugar
2 tablespoons white rum

Cut the pineapple horizontally in thin slices. The slices should look like semi-circles. Combine the sugar and rum in a mixing bowl and add the pineapple to coat. Reserve.

WHITE CHOCOLATE MOUSSE

8 ounces good quality white chocolate, coarsely chopped
1 cup heavy cream, cold
2 tablespoons granulated sugar
juice of 1 lime
7 egg whites, room temperature

1. In a double boiler or bowl over simmering water, melt the chocolate. Set aside to cool.
2. Whip cream until soft peaks form. Add 1 tablespoon of the sugar and all the lime juice; whip until stiff peaks form. Gently fold in the chocolate.

3. In another mixing bowl, beat the egg whites until soft peaks form. Gradually add 1 tablespoon sugar, beating constantly until stiff peaks form.

4. Fold the beaten egg whites into the whipped cream mixture to complete the mousse.

5. Fill the pre-baked tart shell with mousse. Refrigerate for 4 to 6 hours. Arrange pineapple slices in a circular pattern on top and chill for an additional hour before serving.

Serves 6 to 8

Plum Streusel Tart

Susan Feniger and Mary Sue Milliken of City Restaurant

Baking with Fresh Fruit

Since fresh fruit always varies in ripeness, the cooking time will also vary. Use the time in the recipe as a guide. To test for doneness insert the tip of a small knife into the fruit. When the fruit feels soft, the tart is finished.

Don't let the length of this recipe discourage you—it's well worth the effort. The sweet dough makes an unusually crisp crust that combines with the tart's ripe plums and crumbly brown streusel to make a really special dessert. You can use any type of plum. Mary Sue and Susan have been serving this tart since they worked together at their first restaurant, City Café, and customers keep coming back for more.

The sweet dough, almond cream and streusel can be prepared in advance and refrigerated until it's time to assemble.

SWEET DOUGH

6 tablespoons unsalted butter, room temperature
½ cup confectioners' sugar
⅛ teaspoon salt
1 egg
1 cup plus 2 tablespoons all-purpose flour

In a mixing bowl cream the butter, sugar, salt and egg until light and fluffy. Add the flour and beat briefly until combined. Shape into a disk; wrap in plastic wrap and refrigerate for 2 hours or overnight.

ALMOND CREAM

½ cup granulated sugar
½ cup slivered almonds, blanched
6 tablespoons unsalted butter
1 egg
1 egg yolk
1 tablespoon brandy
1 teaspoon vanilla extract

In a food processor combine sugar and almonds and process until nuts are finely ground. Add butter, one tablespoon at a time, processing after each addition until smooth. Add remaining ingredients and process until smooth. Cover and refrigerate until ready to assemble. You can prepare the cream as much as a day in advance.

STREUSEL TOPPING

⅓ cup packed brown sugar
4 tablespoons (½ stick) unsalted butter
⅛ teaspoon salt
⅛ teaspoon cinnamon
¾ cup all-purpose flour

Cream the sugar, butter, salt and cinnamon until light and fluffy. Add the flour; gently mix just until crumbly. Reserve.

6 medium plums, ripe

1. To assemble the tart: Halve, pit and reserve the plums. Roll out dough and line a 10-inch tart pan with removable bottom (page 230). Refrigerate ½ hour.

2. Preheat oven to 350°F. Bake the empty tart shell, topped with pie weights, for 15 minutes (see page 231 for tips on baking blind). Remove from oven, and remove weights. Spread almond cream in tart shell and bake for 10 minutes. Remove from oven and turn heat up to 375°F.

3. Arrange the plum halves cut side down on top of baked almond cream; sprinkle streusel over the top and bake for 20 to 30 minutes or until plums are soft and the crust is golden brown. Serve at room temperature with fresh whipped cream.

Serves 8

Pistachio Torte

Michael Roberts of Trumps

Homemade Bread Crumbs
To make your own bread crumbs,
cut the crusts off white bread,
toast very lightly, and then grind
in a food processor until fine. Two
slices make approximately half a
cup of fine bread crumbs.

Michael developed this recipe as a way to use his favorite nuts—pistachios. During the baking, the egg whites holding the chopped nuts together all but disappear, producing a moist, dense, and crunchy dessert. Macadamia nuts may be substituted and you can use whipped cream as a garnish.

¾ cup (1½ sticks) butter, room temperature
1 cup plus 1 tablespoon granulated sugar
5 eggs, separated
½ cup fine dry bread crumbs
2 cups unsalted pistachio nuts, finely chopped
1 cup lemon curd (garnish) (page 197)

1. Preheat oven to 350°F. Butter and flour a 9-inch springform pan.

2. In a bowl, cream the butter and 1 cup of the sugar together until light and fluffy. Add the egg yolks one at a time, beating well after each addition. Add the bread crumbs and all but a scant ¼ cup of the pistachios. Beat 1 minute to combine. Set aside.

3. In a separate copper or stainless bowl, beat the egg whites until soft peaks form. Add remaining tablespoon of sugar and continue to beat until stiff but not dry peaks form.

4. Whisk one third of the whites into the pistachio mixture to lighten. Then gently fold in the remaining whites.

5. Pour into the prepared pan and smooth top with a spatula. Bake 30 to 35 minutes, or until a cake tester inserted in the center comes out clean.

6. Cool in the pan on a wire rack for 1 hour. Remove the sides of the springform pan and continue to cool *torte* completely.

7. Spread 1 cup of the lemon curd garnish on top and sprinkle with the reserved pistachios.

Serves 8 to 10

Chunky Sweet Potato Pie

Michael Roberts of Trumps

This comforting pie makes a good ending to a Thanksgiving dinner. By cubing the sweet potato rather than mashing it, Michael Roberts adds an interesting new texture to an American classic. You can substitute two cups of toasted pecans for the sweet potato for a good pecan pie.

1 Pâte Sucrée recipe (page 230)

Preheat oven to 375°F. Roll out the *pâte sucrée* and line a 10-inch tart pan with removable bottom (see page 230). Refrigerate for ½ hour.

FILLING

1 large sweet potato (about 1¼ pounds)
4 tablespoons (½ stick) unsalted butter
2 eggs
2 egg yolks
⅔ cup packed dark brown sugar
¾ cup dark corn syrup
1 tablespoon vanilla extract
¼ teaspoon allspice

1. Bake the potato until soft. Set aside to cool. Peel and cut into ½-inch cubes.

2. Bake the empty tart shell with weights for 5 minutes (see page 231 for tips on baking blind). Remove from oven and remove weights.

3. Melt the butter over medium heat until brown sediment forms at the bottom of the pan. Set aside.

4. In a large mixing bowl, beat the eggs, egg yolks, brown sugar, corn syrup, vanilla and allspice until smooth. Pour in the melted butter and mix until combined.

5. Place the potato cubes in the baked tart shell. Pour in the filling and bake for ½ hour or until cake tester inserted in center comes out clean. Serve warm with whipped cream.

Serves 8

Brown Sugar

Brown sugar is less refined and more moist than granulated sugar. Molasses gives it its color and also lends it a richer flavor that works well in cookies, muffins and quickbreads.

When measuring always pack the sugar firmly in dry measuring cups. To minimize lumps, store the sugar in a tightly covered container in a cool, dry place.

Walnut Tart

Celestino Drago of Celestino's

The recipe for this comforting tart comes from Celestino's mother Maria, in Sicily. Celestino suggests you serve it in the wintertime, with a dollop of whipped cream.

1 Pâte Sucrée *recipe (page 230)*

Roll out the dough in a 13-inch circle on a lightly floured board. Line the bottom of a 9-inch springform pan and cut the remaining dough in 2½-inch strips. Line the sides of the pan with the pastry strips, pressing to seal the sides to the bottom.

FILLING

3½ cups walnut halves, toasted
1 cup (2 sticks) unsalted butter, cut in tablespoon-sized pieces
1¼ cups granulated sugar
4 eggs
confectioners' sugar

1. To make the filling: In a food processor fitted with a metal blade, grind 2½ cups of the walnuts until they form a fine powder. Be careful not to overprocess or you'll get a nut butter. Add the butter, sugar and eggs. Process about 30 seconds, until smooth. Reserve.

2. Preheat oven to 300°F.

3. To assemble: Spread ½ cup of the walnut halves over the bottom of the tart shell. Pour in the filling and smooth with a spatula. Bake for 40 to 50 minutes. Set aside to cool on a cake rack for ½ hour.

4. Roughly chop the remaining nuts. Sprinkle the chopped nuts on top of the tart; remove from the pan and dust with confectioners' sugar.

Serves 8

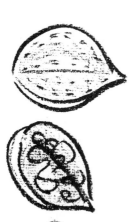

Toasting and Storing Nuts

Toasting or roasting nuts improves their taste and texture. Preheat oven to 350°F. Spread the nuts in one layer on a baking sheet. Bake, shaking the sheet occasionally, until the nuts are golden brown, about ten minutes. Watch the nuts in the oven, as they can burn quickly.

Fresh, shelled nuts can be frozen in a well-sealed container for up to one year. They can be kept in the refrigerator for about a month. Nuts do not have to be defrosted before using in a recipe.

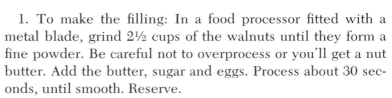

Poached Peaches with Caramel Sauce

Roy Yamaguchi of 385 North

Chef Yamaguchi suggests this rich-tasting warm dessert after a light meal. Nectarines may be substituted for the peaches. See the tip below for the secret of a really smooth caramel.

6 firm peaches
1 bottle Sauternes or other dessert wine
1 vanilla bean

Peel, halve and pit the peaches. In a heavy saucepan combine wine, peaches and vanilla bean. Bring to a simmer and cook for 10 minutes. Remove the peaches with a slotted spoon.

CARAMEL SAUCE

1½ cups granulated sugar
1 pint heavy cream
6 sprigs fresh mint, leaves only (garnish)

1. To make the caramel sauce: In a medium-sized saucepan, over low heat, melt the sugar until it turns dark brown, about 10 minutes. Do not stir while melting. Add the cream and stir constantly until the mixture turns a deep caramel color, about 5 minutes.

2. Spoon some caramel sauce onto each dessert plate and top with two peach halves. Garnish with fresh mint and serve.

Serves 6

Making Caramel

Caramel is easier to make in a light-colored saucepan so that you can see the color changing. Don't stir the sugar while it's melting. If sugar crystals form on the sides of the pan just brush down with a pastry brush dipped in water.

For the richest flavor allow the caramel to take on a deep brown color before adding the cream. Don't be alarmed when the caramel seizes into a hard ball. Simply continue stirring over low heat until the caramel melts again, in about five minutes. The sauce thickens as it cools. Caramel sauce can be refrigerated for up to two weeks.

Baked Apple with Honey Ice Cream

Jean-François Meteigner of L'Orangerie

This is an elegant version of a familiar favorite—baked apples. The exceptionally rich, sweet ice cream is nicely offset by the tartness of the Granny Smith apples and the apricot sauce adds a touch of color. Be sure to leave enough time to make the ice cream. We use a commercial electric ice cream maker but you can, of course, use a hand-cranked machine.

HONEY ICE CREAM

2 cups milk
½ cup honey
8 egg yolks
⅓ cup granulated sugar
½ cup heavy cream, cold

1. Combine the milk and honey and bring to a boil in a medium saucepan. Remove from the heat.

2. Whisk the egg yolks and sugar together in a mixing bowl until the mixture is thick and light colored.

3. Whisk a quarter of the warm milk and honey into the egg mixture. Then pour the egg mixture into the remaining milk mixture. Cook over low heat, stirring constantly, until the mixture coats the back of a wooden spoon. (This will happen quickly.)

4. Remove from heat. Add the cream and stir until cool, about 5 minutes. Cover and refrigerate for 4 to 6 hours.

5. Pour into ice cream maker and follow manufacturer's instructions.

6. After removing from machine, place in container and, if you have the time, allow to freeze for 4 to 6 hours before serving.

BAKED APPLE WITH APRICOT SAUCE

4 large Granny Smith apples, peeled, halved and cored
8 teaspoons granulated sugar
3 tablespoons unsalted butter
1 (17-ounce) can pitted apricots in heavy syrup

Ice Cream Making Tips

To ensure the best tasting homemade ice cream, make certain the custard mixture is thoroughly chilled before pouring it into the ice cream maker. Don't be alarmed if it tastes extremely sweet since chilling always dampens the flavor. After processing in the ice cream maker, it's best to freeze the ice cream for four to six hours before serving, to allow the flavors to blend and ripen. This isn't, however, absolutely necessary.

There are a few things to remember when experimenting with your own additions to a basic ice cream recipe. Don't add more than three to four tablespoons of liquor—alcohol does not freeze, and if you add more than that neither will your ice cream. Alcohol should always be stirred in just before the first refrigeration. Any chips or chunks that you wish to remain solid should be added after processing in the ice cream maker.

1. Preheat oven to 350°F.

2. Place the apples cut side down in a buttered 9 × 13-inch baking dish. Sprinkle each with a teaspoon of sugar and dot top with butter. Bake until soft, about 30 minutes.

3. To make the apricot sauce: Drain and reserve about half of the apricot syrup for another use. In a blender or food processor puree the apricots and the remaining syrup.

4. To serve: Place two apple halves on each dessert plate. Arrange the honey ice cream alongside; drizzle both with the apricot sauce and serve immediately.

Serves 4

Kiwi Spuma with Strawberries and Vanilla Sauce

Celestino Drago of Celestino's

Gelatin

Gelatin gives the *spuma* its spongy consistency. A powdered protein from animal and fish bones, gelatin should always be softened first, by combining it with liquid and allowing it to stand at room temperature until spongy. Applying heat dissolves the gelatin and chilling solidifies the mixture.

The translation for *spuma* is foam—a fitting description for this light, airy dessert. The *spuma*, which is delicious served by itself, may be made a day in advance and refrigerated. Any soft fruit such as cantaloupe, papaya, peaches or nectarines may be substituted in the same proportion as the kiwis. Serve this refreshing cold dessert in the summertime.

4 kiwis, peeled and chopped
1 cup granulated sugar
1 cup milk
2 tablespoons gelatin
4 egg yolks
2 cups heavy cream, cold

1. Have ready ten ½-cup ramekins.
2. Puree the kiwis in a blender or food processor fitted with a metal blade.
3. Combine the kiwis and ½ cup of the sugar in a small saucepan and cook over low heat until the kiwis are soft and the sugar melts, about 3 minutes. Reserve.
4. In another saucepan, combine the milk and gelatin; let stand for 5 minutes to soften. Bring the mixture to a boil and remove from heat.
5. In a mixing bowl, whip the remaining sugar and the egg yolks until the mixture is light-colored and thick.
6. Whisk a quarter of the warm milk and gelatin mixture into the egg yolk mixture. Then pour the remaining milk into the egg mixture and whisk until combined.
7. Stir the pureed kiwis into the milk and egg mixture until combined. Refrigerate for 45 minutes.
8. When the mixture has been chilled, whip the cream until soft peaks form. Whisk one third of the whipped cream into the kiwi mixture to lighten. Fold in the remaining cream in two stages.
9. Pour the completed *spuma* into the ramekins and refrigerate 4 to 6 hours or overnight.

VANILLA SAUCE WITH STRAWBERRY PUREE

2 cups heavy cream
1 vanilla bean
3 tablespoons confectioners' sugar
2 egg yolks
4 large strawberries, hulled
1 tablespoon kirsch
juice of ½ lemon
12 strawberries, sliced (garnish)

1. To make the sauce: Pour the cream into a small saucepan. Split the vanilla bean and scrape the seeds and the bean into the cream. Add 2 tablespoons of the sugar. Bring to a boil and remove from heat.

2. Beat the egg yolks in a medium-sized mixing bowl. Whisk in a quarter of the warm cream mixture. Then combine all the yolks in the remaining cream and return to the stove. Cook over low heat 2 to 3 minutes, until the mixture coats the back of a wooden spoon. Refrigerate until chilled.

3. To make the strawberry puree: Combine the strawberries, kirsch, lemon juice and remaining sugar in a blender. Puree until smooth and strain.

4. To serve: Dip each ramekin in hot water for 30 seconds to loosen contents, or dip a knife in warm water and run it along the inside edge. Invert onto dessert plates and surround with a circle of vanilla sauce.

5. Pour the strawberry puree into a pastry bag with a very fine tip. Pipe a circle in the vanilla sauce and feather with the tip of a small knife or a toothpick. Garnish with sliced strawberries for more color.

Serves 10

Sabayon of Fresh Fruit with Strawberry Sauce

Jean-Pierre Lemanissier of Ma Maison

Dessert Wines

Sauternes, from Bordeaux, are the
best known dessert wines. They
are sweet, mellow white wines
with a honey-like flavor. Chateau
D'Yquem is recognized as the best
Sauternes and is definitely *not*
meant for cooking. Other dessert
wines for cooking or drinking are
Johannisberg Riesling from
California and Alsatian Riesling
from Germany. Look for late
harvest California Riesling for the
sweetest flavor. Serve the better
dessert wines chilled, in small
glasses, along with dessert.

Jean-Pierre came up with this festive dessert for those who generally avoid dessert altogether. *Sabayon*, the French version of *zabaglione*, can be made even lighter by reducing the quantity of sugar or alcohol according to taste. You can also substitute dry white wine for dessert wine and balance it with sugar. Make sure you use ovenproof gratin or custard dishes, since they are placed under the broiler briefly for a burnt sugar crust similar to *crème brûlée*. The strawberry sauce can be served at room temperature or chilled to contrast with the warm custard.

STRAWBERRY SAUCE

1 pint basket strawberries, hulled, or 1 (10-ounce) bag frozen
    strawberries, thawed
3 tablespoons confectioners' sugar
1 teaspoon fresh lemon juice

Combine all the ingredients in a food processor or blender and puree until smooth. Set aside or chill.

SABAYON

4 egg yolks
½ cup Sauternes
½ cup Grand Marnier
⅓ cup granulated sugar
2 cups fresh raspberries, strawberries or blueberries, washed

1. Combine the egg yolks, Sauternes, Grand Marnier and sugar in a large metal bowl. Whisk vigorously until the mixture is smooth and pale and forms a ribbon when the whisk is lifted.

2. Place the bowl over, but not touching, a pan of simmering water. Continue to whisk until the mixture is thick and creamy, about 10 minutes.

3. Preheat the broiler. Divide the berries and place in a single layer in four individual gratin or ovenproof custard dishes. Divide the *sabayon* and pour it over the berries. Place

the dishes on a baking sheet and place under the broiler for 1
minute, until the top just turns golden. Be very careful not to
overcook, since the top can burn quickly.

4. Drizzle each serving with the strawberry sauce and
serve immediately.

Serves 4

City Chocolate with Coffee Crème Anglaise

Susan Feniger and Mary Sue Milliken of City Restaurant

It's not a soufflé. It's not a cake or a frozen dessert. It *is* a chocolate lover's dream. Mary Sue learned this delight in Paris, while she was cooking at the two-star restaurant D'Olympe. Preparation time is about fifteen minutes. See the notes below for tips on separating eggs.

3 tablespoons brandy
1 cup golden raisins
1 pound 2 ounces semisweet chocolate
1¾ cups (3½ sticks) unsalted butter
10 eggs, separated

1. Line a 2-quart mold with enough plastic wrap to hang over the sides about five inches.

2. Warm the brandy over low heat. Remove from heat, stir in raisins and set aside to soak.

3. Chop the chocolate in small pieces and melt with the butter in a double boiler or bowl over simmering water. Remove from heat and whisk until blended in a large mixing bowl. Gently whisk in the raisins and egg yolks.

4. Beat the egg whites until soft peaks form. Stir a cup of the chocolate mixture into the whites. Fold the whites gently into the remaining chocolate mixture in three stages.

5. Pour into the prepared mold, smooth top and cover with plastic wrap touching the top. Refrigerate for 6 hours or overnight.

6. To unmold: Remove the plastic wrap on top. Invert the mold onto a serving platter. The chocolate should release easily when the mold is lifted. Peel off the plastic and smooth the chocolate with a spatula.

COFFEE CRÈME ANGLAISE

2 cups milk
3 teaspoons instant coffee
8 egg yolks
1½ cups granulated sugar
1 teaspoon vanilla extract

Separating Eggs

Cold eggs are easier to separate. Have two bowls ready on a counter. First empty each egg into the palm of your hand. Then, holding your hand over the bowl for collecting whites, shake it from side to side so that the white slides through your fingers into the bowl below and the yolk remains in your palm. Slip the yolks into another bowl. Remember, the slightest trace of yolk in the whites will keep them from rising. For tips on whipping egg whites, see page 200.

1. Mix the milk and coffee in a medium-sized saucepan and bring to a boil. Remove from heat.

2. Beat the egg yolks and sugar until a ribbon forms when the beaters are lifted.

3. Stir a cup of the milk and coffee into the egg mixture. Then pour the egg mixture into the remaining warm milk and cook over low heat for about 5 minutes, until the mixture coats the back of a wooden spoon.

4. Remove from heat and continue to stir until cool, about 5 minutes. Stir in vanilla. Cover and refrigerate until cold.

5. To serve: Spoon some *Crème Anglaise* onto eight dessert plates. Top with a slice of the cold chocolate dessert.

Serves 8

Strawberries with Balsamic Vinegar

Evan Kleiman of Angeli

Balsamic Vinegar

Balsamic vinegar has an unusually dense, sweet taste that is the result of a careful aging process governed by Italian law. It can take as long as fifty years for the vinegar to achieve its brown syrupy consistency and full, round flavor.

Use balsamic vinegar sparingly since the flavor is so concentrated and special. A few drops can enhance the flavor of fresh fruits, salads, cooked vegetables, and even meat and poultry. Always reduce the quantity if substituting balsamic in a recipe that calls for another vinegar.

Combining vinegar and sugar with strawberries may sound like a strange idea, but the taste is divine. The tart, sweet taste of the vinegar paste brings out the berries' natural flavor.

This easy dessert is appropriate after any meal when you don't want to spend extra time in the kitchen. Pass the berries, relax and enjoy the conversation.

strawberries, washed, with stems on
granulated sugar
balsamic vinegar

1. Dry the strawberries and arrange in a serving bowl.
2. On each dessert plate place a tablespoon of sugar. Pour about two teaspoons of vinegar over the mound of sugar and stir to form a paste.
3. Dip the berries into the sugar-vinegar paste and eat. Serve with strong espresso.

Crème Brûlée Supreme

Patrick Jamon of Les Anges

Berries add just the right touch of tartness to this luxuriously rich custard. Make sure you use ovenproof dessert bowls or *gratin* dishes since you'll be placing them under the broiler after the custard chills, to cook the crisp brown crusts. If you become a *crème brûlée* addict, Patrick recommends using a blowtorch for caramelizing the sugar. (Blowtorches are available at most hardware stores.) They make it easier to control the heat. Make sure to leave enough time before serving, since custard needs about five hours to set and chill.

4 cups heavy cream
1 2-inch length vanilla bean
10 egg yolks
1½ cups granulated sugar
1 basket raspberries, blueberries, or strawberries, washed and dried

1. Pour the cream into a heavy saucepan. Split and scrape the vanilla bean and add to the cream. Bring to a boil. Remove from heat, and discard the bean.

2. In a separate bowl, beat the egg yolks and 1 cup of the sugar until pale yellow.

3. Pour a quarter of the hot cream into the yolk mixture, to warm the yolks gradually. Then pour the yolk mixture into the cream in the saucepan and cook over low heat, stirring constantly, until the mixture coats a wooden spoon, about 3 minutes.

4. Divide the berries into 8 portions and scatter them among eight ovenproof dessert bowls. (If using strawberries, they need to be sliced.) Pour the warm custard mixture over the berries and set aside to cool, about 1 hour.

5. Cover and refrigerate at least 4 hours or as long as 2 days.

6. Just before serving, preheat the broiler. Place all the custard dishes on a baking tray. Sprinkle each with a tablespoon of sugar and place under the broiler until the tops are brown, about a minute. Be very careful not to overcook, since the sugar burns quickly. Serve immediately.

Serves 8

Custard Making

To cook the egg yolks without scrambling, in an egg-based sauce or custard such as *creme anglaise* (page 214), *crème brûlée*, caramel custard (page 218) or ice cream, the heat must be applied slowly. A portion of the hot liquid should always be added to the yolks before the two mixtures are combined. The mixture should then be cooked over low heat and stirred constantly. Never bring the mixture to a boil once the yolks are added. You can tell the sauce is done when a finger drawn across the back of a wooden spoon coated with the mixture leaves a clear trail.

Flan

Bruce Marder of Rebecca's

This extremely rich *flan* is closer to a French custard than to the typical Mexican dessert. The high percentage of cream and egg yolks make it wonderfully thick and smooth. Serve *flan* cold, with every last drop of caramel scraped from the molds.

CARAMEL

1 cup granulated sugar

1. In a medium saucepan over medium heat, cook the sugar until it melts and turns dark brown, about 5 minutes. Remember never to stir the sugar when making caramel, and brush down the sugar crystals with a pastry brush dipped in water.
2. Pour the warm caramel into ten ½-cup ramekins and tilt to coat the bottom and sides evenly. Set aside.

CUSTARD

3 cups heavy cream
2 (2-inch) vanilla beans
9 egg yolks
¾ cup granulated sugar

1. Preheat oven to 300°F.
2. Pour the cream into a medium saucepan. Split the vanilla beans lengthwise, scrape the seeds and add the beans and seeds to the cream. Bring just to a boil and immediately remove from heat.
3. Combine the egg yolks and sugar in a mixing bowl. Beat until the mixture is pale and thick.
4. Whisk a quarter of the hot cream into the egg mixture to temper it. Then pour the remaining cream into the eggs and whisk until combined. Discard the vanilla bean and pour the custard into the coated ramekins.

Vanilla Beans

Many chefs prefer the pure taste of vanilla beans to vanilla extract. Vanilla beans, the aged and fermented pods of a yellow orchid plant, are imported from Mexico and Tahiti and are usually about six inches long. Since most recipes call for a two-inch length, break two inches off the bean, split lengthwise and then scrape the small black inner seeds, along with the bean, into the recipe liquid. After you remove the bean from the liqud it can be dried and stored in a sugar canister. The sugar will absorb enough of the vanilla flavor to eliminate the need for vanilla extract in baking recipes.

5. Place the ramekins in two roasting pans. Pour hot water into the pans until it rises halfway up the ramekin's sides, to form a *bain marie* (page 158). Bake for 40 minutes, until the center of the *flan* is just wobbly. Refrigerate 3 to 4 hours.

6. To serve: Release the *flan* by running a knife between the custard and the mold. Invert onto dessert plates and serve cold. *Flan* may be stored in the refrigerator, covered with plastic wrap, for up to a week.

Serves 8

Tiramisu

Antonio Orlando of Valentino

Everybody's spirits are bound to improve after eating this luscious, liquor-soaked dessert. *Tiramisu* literally means "lift me up," which is exactly what the Marsala wine and coffee liqueur do.

This wonderful, special occasion dessert is surprisingly easy to make. Antonio suggests you prepare it a day in advance to chill properly. He serves it in small glass bowls or deep wineglasses so that guests can appreciate the lovely layers of whipped *mascarpone* and ladyfingers. You can also use a one-and-a-half-quart container—a trifle dish or glass salad bowl would be fine—or individual-sized serving dishes to prepare this dessert.

6 egg yolks
1 cup granulated sugar
½ cup Marsala
1½ pounds mascarpone *or cream cheese, softened*
2 cups warm espresso
1 cup Kahlua or coffee liqueur
2 (3-ounce) boxes ladyfingers

1. With an electric mixer, whip the egg yolks, sugar and Marsala together until the mixture is light and fluffy, about 2 minutes. Cut cream cheese into 1-inch squares and gradually add to egg mixture, beating continuously, until mixture is thick and smooth, about 10 minutes.

2. In another bowl, mix the espresso and coffee liqueur. Dip the ladyfingers, one at a time, in the coffee mixture and line the bottom of the serving bowl with them. Then spoon half of the cheese mixture on top of the ladyfingers. Follow with another layer of dipped ladyfingers and top with the remaining cheese mixture. Cover and refrigerate for a minimum of 1 hour before serving.

Serves 8 to 10

Zabaglione with Berries and Cream

Celestino Drago of Celestino's

Never underestimate the power of a good dessert. In his native Italy, Celestino reports that *zabaglione* is prescribed for honeymooners and sick children as a restorative. Though we can't promise any miracles, we do think *zabaglione* is delicious served warm or chilled with whatever berries are in season. The whipped cream is optional.

3 large egg yolks
½ cup plus 1 tablespoon granulated sugar
7 tablespoons sweet Marsala
½ cup heavy cream, cold
1 pint basket strawberries, hulled and quartered

1. In a bowl over but not touching simmering water, whisk together the egg yolks and ½ cup of the sugar until smooth and pale. Add the Marsala, one tablespoon at a time, whisking thoroughly between additions. Continue to cook, whisking constantly, for 10 minutes or until the mixture is thick and creamy. Remove from heat and reserve. The *zabaglione* may be kept in the refrigerator for about a day.

2. Whip the cream with the remaining sugar until soft peaks form.

3. To serve: Divide the *zabaglione* among four wineglasses or glass bowls. Divide the berries and layer on top. Top with whipped cream and serve.

Serves 4

Marsala and Fortified Wines

Marsala is a fortified wine that comes from Sicily. It has a higher alcohol content than ordinary wine, about 17 percent, due to the brandy that has been added.

All the fortified wines are popular for cooking because they add a more pronounced flavor. As a general rule use about half as much if substituting a fortified wine for another type. The other fortified wines are Madeira, port, sherry and vermouth.

BASICS

Chicken Stock

Chicken stock is the base for innumerable soups and sauces. By making your own you can avoid the overly salted and flavored commercial brands, which become even saltier as they are reduced.

1 pound chicken bones (bones from about 3 whole breasts)
2 celery stalks, chopped
2 carrots, peeled and chopped
1 onion, choppd
1 bay leaf
10 cups water

1. Combine all the ingredients in a large saucepan and bring to a boil. Skim the foam off the top, reduce to a simmer and cook, uncovered, about 2 hours.

2. Strain the mixture, discarding the solids, and refrigerate for 1 hour. When a layer of fat forms at the top, skim and discard. The stock can be stored, in a covered container in the refrigerator, for 4 to 5 days, or frozen indefinitely. Freeze in small batches for convenience.

Yields 2 quarts

Variations: For double strength chicken stock, excellent for sauce-making, substitute chicken stock for the 10 cups of water and follow the same method.

For homemade chicken soup, add diced vegetables and chopped, cooked chicken to the stock and simmer until the vegetables are soft.

Fish Stock

The bones of any white fish are good for making fish stock. Just avoid oily fishes like salmon, mackerel and tuna, and don't use an aluminum stockpot, because a chemical reaction will cause the stock to turn gray.

2 tablespoons unsalted butter
1 leek, white and green parts, cleaned and chopped
1 carrot, peeled and chopped
1/2 onion, chopped
2 pounds fish bones, cut into 2-inch pieces

1 cup dry white wine
6 cups water
bouquet garni

1. Melt the butter in a large stockpot over medium heat. Cook the leek, carrot and onion until soft, about 3 minutes.

2. Add the bones and sauté about 5 minutes. Pour in the wine and water. Add the *bouquet garni* and bring the mixture to a boil. Skim the foam off the top, reduce to a simmer and cook, uncovered, for about 40 minutes.

3. Strain the mixture, discarding the solids, and set aside to cool. Refrigerate about 2 hours and then skim and discard the layer of fat that has formed at the top. Fish stock can be stored, in a sealed container in the refrigerator, for 3 to 4 days, or frozen up to a month. Freeze in small batches for convenience.

Yields 6 cups

Bouquet Garni

This small sack of herbs and spices adds a subtle flavor to long simmering soups and stews. Always remember to remove before serving.

3 sprigs fresh parsley
2 sprigs fresh thyme
1 bay leaf
4 black peppercorns

Place the ingredients in a small square of cheesecloth and tie it with a string.

Veal Stock

Veal stock has a subtler flavor than stock derived from beef bones. It forms the base for most of the dark sauces in this book. Ask your butcher to cut through the bones so the centers are exposed, to better release their valuable gelatin. Shank and shoulder bones are best. The simmering stockpot need not be watched. Renée recommends setting it up for an overnight simmer before bedtime.

10 pounds veal bones
3 onions, halved
3 tablespoons unsalted butter
4 carrots, peeled and chopped
2 leeks, white and green parts, cleaned and chopped
2 cups dry white wine
4 quarts water
bouquet garni *(page 225)*

1. Preheat oven to 400°F.

2. Place the bones and onions on a large baking sheet lined with aluminum foil and bake for 45 minutes, until brown.

3. In the meantime, in a large stockpot, melt the butter over medium heat. Sauté the carrots and leeks until brown, about 15 minutes.

4. When the bones are well browned, remove from the oven and pour off the excess grease. Add the bones and onions to the mixture in the stockpot; turn the heat to high and add 1 cup of wine. Cook for 5 minutes to caramelize the juices at the bottom of the pot. Pour in the second cup of wine, scraping the bottom to release the brown bits and cook an additional 5 minutes.

5. Pour in the water to cover; add the *bouquet garni* and bring to a boil. Skim the foam off the top; reduce to a simmer and cook for 8 to 12 hours, uncovered.

6. Strain the stock, discarding the solids, and set aside to cool to room temperature. Refrigerate about 4 hours. Then remove and discard the layer of fat that has formed at the top. Veal stock should be dark brown in color and gelatinous in texture when cold. The stock can be stored, in a sealed container in the refrigerator, for 4 to 5 days, or frozen indefinitely. Freeze in small batches for convenience.

Yields 10 cups

Marinara Sauce

We never run out of uses for this simple tomato sauce. You can serve it on pasta or pizza as well as on fried eggplant or zucchini or a simple grilled fish entrée. Please taste it before adding the optional sugar. Ripe Italian plum tomatoes might be sweet enough.

3 tablespoons olive oil
1 large onion, finely chopped
3 garlic cloves, finely minced
3 pounds Italian plum tomatoes, peeled, seeded and coarsely
  chopped (page 19), or 32 ounces canned plum tomatoes
1 (6-ounce) can tomato paste
1 tablespoon dried thyme, crumbled
1 tablespoon dried oregano, crumbled
1 bay leaf
1 teaspoon granulated sugar (optional)
10 fresh basil leaves, cut into strips
salt and freshly ground pepper to taste

1. Heat the oil in a medium-sized skillet over medium heat. Add the onions and cook until soft, about 5 minutes. Add the garlic and cook an additional minute, stirring occasionally to avoid browning the garlic.

2. Add the tomatoes, tomato paste, thyme, oregano, bay leaf and sugar, if necessary. Bring the mixture to a boil and reduce to a simmer. Cook for 1 hour, uncovered, stirring occasionally.

3. Remove the bay leaf, stir in the basil and season with salt and pepper to taste. Simmer an additional 5 minutes and serve or store in sealed containers in the refrigerator or freezer.

Yields 3 cups

Variations:
If you prefer a smoother sauce, puree in a food processor or blender before adding the basil and final seasonings.

If you like mushrooms in your sauce, slice them thinly and add for an additional 15 minutes at the end.

To add Italian sausage, remove the meat from the casings, and sauté in a separate pan until just done. Add to the sauce for the last 5 minutes.

Homemade Mayonnaise

We like the mild flavor of safflower oil for mayonnaise, but you can use almost any cooking oil. Use olive oil for a more pungent taste or vegetable or corn oil if you prefer a neutral-flavored mayonnaise.

2 egg yolks
2 tablespoons fresh lemon juice
1 tablespoon Dijon mustard
1½ cups safflower oil
½ teaspoon salt
⅛ teaspoon white pepper

1. Combine egg yolks, lemon juice and mustard in a food processor and process about 15 seconds.

2. With the machine running, gradually add the oil through the feed tube in a slow, steady stream. When all the oil has been added, add salt and pepper and process briefly to combine. Mayonnaise may be stored in a sealed container in the refrigerator for a week. Don't freeze.

Yields 2 cups

Variations:

Add a tablespoon of chopped fresh herbs such as rosemary, basil or tarragon along with the salt and pepper, for herb-flavored mayonnaise.

For *aioli* mayonnaise, first drop 8 garlic cloves into the feed tube, with the machine running. Then follow the same procedure as for basic mayonnaise.

Basic Vinaigrette

The rule of thumb for mixing your own salad dressing is three parts oil to one part vinegar. The rest depends on your creativity.

1 tablespoon Dijon mustard
¼ cup sherry vinegar
¼ cup extra virgin olive oil
½ cup safflower oil
salt and freshly ground pepper to taste

1. Whisk together the mustard and vinegar in a mixing bowl.

2. Drizzle in the oils, whisking constantly to combine. Add salt and pepper to taste. Vinaigrette may be stored in a sealed container in the refrigerator for 5 to 6 days. Whisk to recombine before serving.

Yields 1 cup

Variations:

Make herb garlic dressing by adding 1 minced garlic clove to the mustard and vinegar, adding the oil, then adding 2 tablespoons each of fresh chopped basil and chives, and the salt and pepper.

Substitute raspberry wine vinegar and walnut oil for a fruity vinaigrette to dress a grilled duck or chicken salad.

Egg Pasta

While many of the restaurants serving fresh pasta roll out the dough by hand with a rolling pin, we think most home cooks will prefer our method. Instead of a difficult chore, the food processor and pasta machine make homemade pasta an interesting pastime for long weekends. By the way, young children make excellent pasta machine operators.

4 cups all-purpose flour
3 eggs
1 teaspoon salt
1 teaspoon vegetable oil
½ cup water

1. Place the flour in the bowl of a food processor. In a separate mixing bowl beat the eggs, salt and oil until combined. With the machine running, add the egg mixture to the flour. Gradually add the water through the feed tube until the dough forms small moist beads. The beads should stick together when pressed. The amount of water will vary according to the flour's ability to absorb.

2. Remove the dough and knead on a lightly floured board until the dough is smooth and elastic, about 2 minutes. Wrap in plastic and set aside, at room temperature, for 10 minutes. Divide dough in four parts; wrap three of them in plastic.

3. To knead the dough: Flatten the unwrapped portion of dough by hand and, with the machine at the widest setting, roll it through once. Fold the dough in half, turn it, and roll it again through the same setting. Repeat this procedure ten times, folding and turning each time, until the dough is perfectly smooth. Sprinkle lightly with flour if the dough is sticky.

4. To stretch the dough: With the machine at the next narrower setting, roll the dough through twice. Reduce the set-

ting, rolling the dough through twice at each setting until you reach the next to the last setting. It is not necessary to fold the dough while stretching. If the lengths become unwieldy, trim them into shorter pieces.

5. If you are stuffing the pasta, immediately proceed with the recipe. If you are making long noodles, lay the pasta on lightly floured counters to dry for about 10 minutes. Fresh, dry pasta should feel as smooth as suede before you cut it. The strands will stick if not properly dried. See page 43 for additional storing and cooking instructions.

Yields 2 pounds or 8 servings

Pâte Sucrée

This sweet pastry is perfect for any fruit tart or pie. The key to preparing light, flaky pie crust is keeping the butter from fully combining with the flour. To do this, always start with cold butter. Be careful not to overprocess when mixing. Handle the dough as little as possible. Renée suggests always having a sheet of plastic wrap between your fingers and the dough so the heat of your hands doesn't melt the butter.

Marble and formica make the best rolling surfaces since they retain the cold. All of the tart recipes in this book call for tart pans with removable bottoms for easy tart removal. If your tin is the blackened type, reduce the heat by 25°F since these pans absorb more heat and darken the crust. All that said, relax, follow these step-by-step instructions and enjoy beautiful tarts and pies! Remember, you'll have to start this about 1¾ hours before you need it, since it needs about an hour of refrigeration and then a half hour to soften.

2 cups less 2 tablespoons all-purpose flour
3½ tablespoons granulated sugar
¾ cup (1½ sticks) unsalted butter, cold
2 egg yolks
½ teaspoon vanilla extract

1. Slice the butter and combine with the flour and sugar in a food processor fitted with a metal blade. Process until the mixture has a mealy texture, about 30 seconds.

2. Combine the egg yolks and vanilla in a small bowl. Gradually pour through the feed tube, pulsing 15 to 20 times to

combine with other ingredients. When the dough begins to clump together and form little balls, it is done. *The mixture should not form a ball around the blade.*

3. Wrap the dough in plastic and shape it into a 1 inch thick by 6-inch round disk. Refrigerate a minimum of an hour or as long as a day. Well-wrapped *pâte sucrée* may be frozen indefinitely.

4. To roll out: Let the dough sit at room temperature for half an hour to soften. Divide the disk in half. On a lightly floured board, working from the center out, roll each disk to ⅛-inch thickness. Keep making slight turns with the dough to prevent it from sticking, and flour the rolling pin three or four times, if necessary.

5. To line the tart pan: Tuck one end of the dough around the pin and loosely wrap it, so the pin can carry the dough to the tart pan. Unroll the dough over the pan and press it evenly into the bottom and sides of the pan, so that it extends about half an inch. Remove any excess dough. To crimp the edges, press the dough between the flutes with your fingers. Any tears in the dough can be patched with the extra dough from the edges. Refrigerate 15 minutes to prevent shrinkage.

6. To bake the empty tart shell (baking blind): Preheat oven to 425°F. Press the dough into the pan as in step 5. Prick in several places with the tines of a fork and then cover with a square of parchment paper or aluminum foil an inch larger than the pan. Place pie weights, rice or beans evenly over the paper. Bake for 10 minutes. Remove the paper and weights (rice or beans should be saved for other pies) and bake for an additional 10 minutes, until nicely browned.

Yields two 9-inch tart shells or one 10-inch shell plus two miniatures or cookies

Pâte Brisée

This sugarless pastry is excellent for savory tarts or quiches. The method is much the same as that used for *pâte sucrée*.

8 tablespoons (1 stick) unsalted butter, cold
1⅓ cups all-purpose flour
½ teaspoon salt
4 tablespoons ice water

1. Slice the butter and combine with the flour and salt in a food processor. Process until the mixture has a mealy texture, about 30 seconds.

2. Gradually add the ice water through the feed tube, while processing with short pulses. When the dough begins to clump together, after about 10 pulses, it is done. Dough should not form a ball over the blade.

3. Wrap the dough in plastic and shape it into a 1-inch thick by 5-inch round disk. For storing, rolling and baking, follow the same procedure as for *pâte sucrée* (page 230).

Yields one 10-inch tart shell or one 9-inch shell plus two miniatures

Puff Pastry

Puff pastry, or *pâte feuilletée*, is a challenge to produce. The incredibly thin, crisp layers rise the way they do as a result of a meticulous process of combining pastry dough, or the *détrempe*, with a block of cold butter. When the completed cold dough is placed inside a hot oven, the water in the butter releases steam, pushing the layers of dough upward. Ma Cuisine's recipe comes from La Tour D'Argent, where Renée apprenticed one summer. Bear in mind that because the dough has to rest during its preparation, you should begin at least three hours before you need it.

DÉTREMPE

3⅓ cups all-purpose flour
1 teaspoon salt
4 tablespoons (½ stick) unsalted butter, melted and cooled to room temperature
1 egg yolk
¾ cup cold water

1. Combine the flour and salt in a food processor fitted with a metal blade. With the machine running, add the butter and egg yolk. Gradually add the water through the feed tube until the dough begins to clump together and form a soft ball.

2. With plastic wrap between your hands and the dough, shape the dough into a 1½-inch thick by 6-inch round disk. Remove plastic, and with a sharp knife score a half-inch deep

A Few Tips

Don't attempt puff pastry in a hot kitchen. Unless you are very experienced, the butter will soften in the time it takes to complete the turns. If the butter is softening, return to the refrigerator until hard again.

If you must flour the board to prevent sticking, brush off the excess so that the proportion of flour to butter doesn't change drastically.

As you are folding and turning, remember that the dough's seam should always remain perpendicular to you. And the rolling is always forward and back, never from side to side.

To achieve the best height:
• Use a sharp knife and make a clean cut when cutting the pastry. A sawing or dragging motion will cause the layers to compress.
• When rolling out the dough, stop just short of the edges to avoid sealing them.
• If the recipe calls for an egg wash before baking, be careful not to let the egg drip over the pastry's sides, sealing them.
• It's best to refrigerate the dough one last time before baking, while the oven is reheating at the highest setting.
• Arrange the oven rack in the lower third of the oven, transfer the cold dough to a very hot oven, reduce the temperature to the recipe's specifications and watch the fruits of your labor rise.

X in the center of the disk to relax the gluten. Wrap in plastic and refrigerate 1 hour, while making the butter block.

BUTTER BLOCK

1 pound (4 sticks) unsalted butter, cold
1 1/3 cups all-purpose flour

1. Slice the butter and combine with the flour in a food processor fitted with a metal blade. Process until a ball is formed around the blade, about 30 seconds.

2. Wrap in plastic and flatten the mixture by hand into a 6-inch square, 1-inch thick. Refrigerate 45 minutes.

3. To roll out and assemble the two parts: On a cold, lightly floured surface, preferably marble, place the dough, with the scored side up. Using a heavy rolling pin, roll the dough from the center out in four directions, to quarter-inch thickness, leaving the area in the middle, where the X is, slightly thicker. The dough should resemble a four-leaf clover.

4. Center the butter block on the dough and fold the four sides over, completely enclosing the butter. Brush off any excess flour as you are folding. Pound on the block with a rolling pin to flatten slightly, and roll the dough out to form a 6-inch by 18-inch rectangle. Fold the rectangle in thirds, as you would a business letter, to form a 6-× 6-inch square. Turn the folded dough clockwise a quarter turn. You have now completed one turn. To make the second turn, roll it out again in a rectangle. Fold the rectangle in thirds again. With your finger, press two dots into the dough, wrap it in plastic and refrigerate for half an hour to chill the butter. The two dots are a reminder that the dough has been rolled and folded twice. Puff pastry has a total of six turns.

5. Roll, fold and turn the dough two more times; press the dough with four dots, wrap, and refrigerate for half an hour. Repeat the same procedure two more times, for a total of six, and the puff pastry is complete. It can be stored, wrapped in plastic in the refrigerator for four to five days or frozen for up to three months.

Yields 3 pounds

Renée's Hot Fudge Sauce

Renée's recipe is the quintessential hot fudge sauce, developed after exhaustive and glorious weeks of testing and tasting over countless bowls of Häagen Dazs vanilla.

5 tablespoons unsalted butter
4 ounces bittersweet chocolate, roughly chopped
½ cup granulated sugar
⅔ cup heavy cream
pinch of salt
1 teaspoon vanilla extract

1. Combine the butter, chocolate, sugar and cream in a heavy saucepan. Place over low heat and cook until the butter and chocolate are melted. Whisk until smooth.
2. Turn the heat to medium-high and bring the mixture to a boil, stirring constantly.
3. Remove from heat. Stir in the salt and vanilla and serve immediately. Hot fudge sauce may be stored, in a sealed container, in the refrigerator for up to 2 weeks. Reheat over low heat, stirring constantly.

Yields 1½ cups

Frangipane

This ground almond paste is wonderful spread on slices of *brioche* or croissant, baked at 400°F until golden brown, and then sprinkled with powdered sugar. It is also good as a filling for fruit tarts and Raspberry-Almond French Toast (page 178). *Frangipane* keeps in the refrigerator for about a week.

1 cup whole shelled almonds
1 tablespoon all-purpose flour
8 tablespoons (1 stick) unsalted butter, room temperature
½ cup granulated sugar
2 egg yolks
1½ teaspoons almond extract
pinch of salt

1. Combine the almonds and flour in a food processor and process until finely ground. Transfer to a bowl and reserve.

2. Process the butter in a food processor until smooth. Add the sugar, egg yolks, almond extract and salt. Process until fluffy, about 2 minutes. Add the ground almonds and combine, with about 10 short pulses. Refrigerate until firm enough to spread, about 1 hour.

Yields 1 cup

INDEX

P

Q

R

Rabbit, 137
saddle of, stuffed, with
mustard sauce, 137–38
stock, 137
Raspberry
almond French toast, 178
sauce, lemon waffles
with, 181–82
-walnut dressing, 81
Ratatouille, cold, 163
Red butter sauce, 142–43
Red peppers, *see* Pepper(s)
Relish, cranberry, 112
Renée's hot fudge sauce,
234
Rice
basmati, 46
in China, 47
fried, Mon Kee, 47
rinsing, 46
risotto verde, 48
Risotto verde, 48
Roasting tips, 111
Rolls, orange pecan, 65–66
Roquefort, 78
sauce, lamb tenderloin
with, 131–32
Roux, 41

S

Sabayon of fresh fruit with
strawberry sauce, 212–
13
Saffron
sauce, scallop salad with,
95–96

steamed mussels with
tomato and, 12–13
Salad dressing
for Asian grilled duck
salad, 85
Caesar, 97
Gorgonzola, 78–79
herb garlic, 229
honey-mustard, 89
Oriental, 94
raspberry-walnut, 81
tomato, 165–66
tuna, 101–2
See also Mayonnaise;
Vinaigrette
Salad greens, 228
Salads, 69–102
Asian grilled duck, 84–
85
California vegetable,
with avocado
vinaigrette, 72–73
chicken
with Gorgonzola
cheese, 78–79
grilled, and goat
cheese, 76–77
Ma Maison, 74–75
smoked, with julienned
vegetables, 82–83
stuffed breasts, with
raspberry-walnut
dressing, 80–81
of chopped veal, olives
and tomatoes, 101–2
garden, with asparagus
sauce, 70–71
grapefruit, with fresh
mint, 87
lobster and orange 90–91
Oriental pork, 93–94
panzanella, 92

with poached eggs and
hot bacon bits, 86
proper way to dress, 88
scallop
with saffron sauce, 95–
96
with spinach and
roasted peppers, 97–98
shrimp, with basil
vinaigrette dressing,
99–100
wild mountain, with
honey-mustard
dressing, 88–89
Salmon
poached, in tomato and
sorrel sauce, 146
sauce, bow tie pasta in,
36
and sea bass, woven
Navajo style, with
green chile butter
sauce, 144–45
seared, with herbed corn
and red butter sauce,
142–43
tartare with smoked
salmon sauce, 18
See also Smoked salmon
Salsa
jalapeño cilantro, 76
tomatillo, 15
tomato, 25
Sandwiches
grilled lamb and red
pepper, 176
smoked chicken and
prune, 171
Sauce(s)
apricot, 208–9
asparagus, 70–71
béchamel, 41

245